FOREIGN AFFAIRS
Special Collection

Foreign Affairs Special Collection: Clueless in Gaza

Editor Gideon Rose Introduces the Collection

When the latest round of Middle East peace talks collapsed earlier this year, experienced observers knew that it was only a matter of time before the Israeli-Palestinian conflict blew up once again. And sure enough, a few weeks later, it did. The war has died down since then, but this is a story without a happy ending—another chapter in a never-ending struggle. We've brought together high-level commentary by our authors to provide the context, background, and forward-looking analysis that you need to understand the issues involved.

ON ISRAELI STRATEGY:
Hussein Ibish, a senior fellow at the Brookings Institution, explains Israeli Prime Minister Benjamin Netanyahu's strategy for the war in Gaza.

ON HAMAS' ROCKETS:
Mark Perry, an expert on Palestine, writes that Hamas' rockets are incapable of inflicting mass casualties, which makes Israel's military response to them counterproductive.

ON TUNNELS:
Military historian Arthur Herman explains the long history of using tunnels during war—and why they're so effective.

ON THE FUTURE:
Martin Indyk argues that an international trusteeship for Palestine is the only way to shore up fundamentally weak Palestinian governing institutions and build peace in the long term.

Visit ForeignAffairs.com for more on these topics—and all our other great content.

Israel Banks on a Fence

Yuval Elizur

Peace Through Separation

Recent public opinion polls show that a growing number of Israeli citizens support a two-state solution to the Israeli-Palestinian conflict, while also believing that a total separation of the two peoples is necessary—at least for a time. Separation is now seen as so important that a majority of Israelis even favor doing it unilaterally if need be. In the wake of the second intifada, much of the population has lost faith in negotiated solutions.

The same opinion polls indicate that most Israelis now believe that the fastest and most efficient way to achieve the separation they desire is through the erection of an electronic fence, and such a barrier is in fact already under construction. The fence will inevitably lead (at least initially) to an economic divorce between Israel and Palestine, which will create hardship for both sides until each economy becomes more self-reliant. But both peoples seem to favor such a course over living in a binational state that they could not be sure of controlling.

A growing number of Israelis now realize that demographic imperatives, and not just basic justice, dictate a two-state solution. The drastic decline in Jewish immigration to Israel in recent years—as well as the very high birthrate among Palestinians—has led population experts to predict that by 2020 or shortly thereafter, there will be an Arab majority in all the territory between the Mediterranean and the Jordan River. At that point, the land will cease to be "Jewish."

YUVAL ELIZUR is a veteran Jerusalem-born journalist and author. He was Deputy Editor of Maariv, Israel's mass circulation daily, as well as Israel Correspondent for *The Washington Post* and *The Boston Globe*.

Israel's politicians have been quick to take note of the growing support for a complete division between the two peoples. Amram Mitzna, the new leader of the Labor Party, has called for an immediate Israeli withdrawal from Gaza and most of the West Bank, together with the building of a wall. His opponent, Prime Minister Ariel Sharon, has also backed construction of the fence (albeit reluctantly, and in the wake of mounting public pressure), but without letting go of the settlements.

The preference for unilateral separation over a negotiated agreement is the result of the reluctance of leaders on both sides to strive for a two-state solution. Neither Sharon nor Yasir Arafat seems to want such a result. The two men realize that a fence will be more than just a physical barrier. It will also play a psychological role, preparing their nations for separation from which there will be no return. Both Sharon and Arafat have therefore helped torpedo negotiations: on several occasions when talks seemed imminent, Sharon took steps that fanned the flames of Arab animosity and sabotaged Palestinian attempts at reform (including efforts to replace Arafat with leaders more inclined to make peace). And Arafat, for his part, has secretly—and at times not so secretly—encouraged terrorism against Israel, despite making repeated promises to rein in Hamas and other rejectionist groups.

There is another reason, less obvious but perhaps more powerful, why recent attempts to restart the negotiations between Israelis and Palestinians have failed: the legacy of the now-defunct Oslo peace process. Oslo allowed both sides to delay resolving fundamental issues such as land and water rights, without giving Israelis total security or the Palestinians a state. So much damage was done to both sides, and confidence was so undermined, that today all the alternatives to separation appear to have been discredited.

But separation, even unilateral separation carried out by Israel, should not be regarded simply as an act of frustration in the absence of negotiation. It could well be the best hope for peace in the region. Although it may be painful initially—indeed, the economic dislocation may be severe—separation should ultimately profit both sides. And it will help create the conditions that may ultimately lead to a final negotiated peace between Israel and the Palestinians.

The Oslo Error

It has now become obvious that Oslo—which represented an attempt to avoid the arduous and dangerous process of negotiating a detailed, final peace plan between Israel and the Palestinians—was, in part, a blunder. The 1993 declaration of principles allowed both sides to ignore many of its terms: in the case of the Israelis, by continuing their massive effort to establish settlements in the West Bank and Gaza, and in the case of the Palestinians, by disregarding their commitment not to arm themselves or engage in violence.

Observers usually blame the "humiliation of occupation" endured by the Palestinians for the savage terrorism they have mounted in the years since the Oslo agreement was signed. Although psychological factors may indeed have played a major role in these events, however, it was the negotiators' failure to grapple with some of the issues underlying the conflict that has been a much more important trigger for the bloodshed than many experts are willing to admit.

Oslo was premised on the principle of "sliding into peace." Its negotiators were convinced that the more both sides enjoyed the fruits of the initial agreement, the more flexible they would become regarding what were once thought the most divisive questions: namely, settlements, borders, Jerusalem, and control of the holy places. The Oslo agreement was also based on the idea of an eventual economic union between Israel and the future Palestinian state.

All of these premises, however, have turned out to be flawed. The idea of an economic union is an oversimplified concept that sounds good to politicians and theoretical economists but is highly problematic in practice. The notion is so attractive that even the un's 1947 partition resolution called for the establishment of two states joined together by just such a union. The idea was that Palestine, as a territorial unit, was too small to justify the existence of

3

two separate economies. Unfortunately, plans for an economic union ignore the regional realities of the past 100 years: the mutual suspicions, the uneven economic potential, and above all, the failure of Israelis and Palestinians to ever agree on how to divide their meager natural resources such as land and water—resources that both sides regard as essential to their very existence.

Breathing Room

The struggle over land has always been the core of the conflict between Jews and Arabs in Palestine. Today that legacy takes the form of bitter resentment on both sides—resentment that Oslo ignored but that must be addressed by any final settlement.

Although they lacked political sovereignty under Ottoman and British rule, Palestine's Arabs felt some security and even a sense of national identity for as long as they held control over most of the land. This control began to slip and local anxiety increased, however, when Arab landowners, some of whom lived outside Palestine, began selling large tracts of land to Jewish settlers. In some cases, Arab tenant farmers were unceremoniously evicted from plots their families had tilled for generations.

At the time, the economic potential of a country in such an arid part of the world was thought to depend on the quantity of arable land available for fallow farming. Based on this concept, the British Mandatory Authority adopted "absorptive capacity"—namely, the amount of additional farmers the local agriculture could support—as a yardstick to determine how much additional Jewish immigration to allow into Palestine. In 1939, with the land question becoming ever more explosive, the British issued a regulation preventing Jews from purchasing land in certain areas of Palestine. This discriminatory act was a failure, however: it not only infuriated Jews, who compared it to the antisemitic Nuremberg Laws adopted in Germany four years earlier, but it also encouraged Arab nationalists to increase their demands. No similar discriminatory legislation was ever passed again.

The establishment of Israel in 1948 seemed finally to grant the Jews a unique opportunity to fulfill their aspirations for massive land acquisition. The newly created Israel Land Authority was given the task of administering the hundreds of villages abandoned by their Arab inhabitants, as well as all land owned by the Israeli government and the Jewish National Fund (JNF). Although the JNF contributed no more than 18 percent of the land controlled by the Israel Land Authority today, it still maintains 50 percent control in all Land Authority bodies. This dominant position has resulted in gross underrepresentation of Israeli Arabs (who make up 20 percent of Israel's population) and much discrimination against them—especially in the expropriation of land for government purposes.

Israel has also expropriated land over the years for the establishment of settlements in the West Bank and Gaza, invoking the right of eminent domain. As a result, in the Gaza Strip—which has one of the highest population densities in the world—about a dozen Israeli settlements now occupy 40 percent of the arable land. Given this long and bitter legacy, it is hardly surprising that, from the Palestinian perspective, Israel will have to do more than remove its settlements before a final peace can be reached. The question of land rights was one of many major subjects that the Oslo agreement intentionally avoided, and any future agreement between Israel and Palestine will have to resolve it conclusively.

Dividing the Waters

Although Israel is part of the "fertile crescent" that stretches from Mesopotamia to the Nile, the shortage of water has always been a dominant factor in the existence of the local population. The Bible tells of conflict between Abraham and Avimelech, the king of Grar, over wells needed for their sheep and goats, and the situation has hardly improved in the centuries since. Indeed, things were little better a hundred years ago—even though the population was much smaller then, the standard of living (and thus the level of water consumption) much lower, and agriculture more primitive.

Once they arrived in Palestine, Jewish settlers dug wells, built water reservoirs, and, in the 1950s, undertook ambitious irrigation projects, bringing water from the Sea of Galilee in the north to the Negev Desert in the south. Although this may have allowed Israel to partially realize the Zionist dream of "making the desert bloom," it has now become evident that the pumping was overambitious and grossly wasteful. Israeli water experts overestimated the size of the country's reserves—in part due to political pressure from Israel's powerful agriculture lobby, which insisted on using precious water for thirsty crops such as cotton. The situation was then exacerbated in 1967, when Israel gained control over the West Bank and Gaza and began to overexploit the mountain aquifer in the center of the country. Photographs from the era show Israeli children splashing around in swimming pools in some of the newly established settlements, while in towns such as Hebron, the pipes began to run dry in summer and water for basic human needs had to be supplied to households by tankers (a situation that continues to this day).

The declining cost of desalinated sea water now seems to be the only hope for Israel and its neighbors to solve their permanent water shortage. Several desalination plants are already under construction in Israel, and these may partially alleviate the crisis. Yet any progress toward peace between Israel and the Palestinians will require a detailed agreement for the equitable division of all available sources of water, starting with the Hatzbani River and its tributaries in Lebanon, the sources of the Jordan River in Syria, and all water presently pumped from aquifers in Israel and the West Bank. Oslo, unfortunately, ignored these water questions. Now a formal agreement, or at least an understanding in principle, on how to allocate the region's insufficient water supply will be critical in order to reach a political solution between Israel and the Palestinians.

Sins of Omission

As mentioned above, the Oslo agreement was based on the concept of "sliding into peace"—a concept that was used by both sides to justify avoiding controversial questions such as borders, Jerusalem, settlements, land and water rights, and the future economic, social, and political relations between the two states of Palestine. Such matters were either erroneously thought out or not thought out at all.

The most blatant of these sins of omission was the Paris agreement of April 1994, which outlined the future economic relations between Israel and the newly formed Palestinian Authority (PA). Although the agreement was termed "temporary," its signatories knew very well that it would set the pattern for all future relations between the two states. Since Israel insisted that there should be no border demarcation between areas under its control and those ruled by the Palestinians, there was no way to avoid massive smuggling of goods between the various zones. Therefore, different rates of import duties and excise taxes had to be avoided.

The Palestinians reluctantly agreed that Israel would collect customs and excise duties on their behalf. Since these taxes were to become the PA's main source of revenue (income tax collection in the Palestinian territories is negligible), the agreement drastically reduced the Palestinians' control over their economy. The agreement also allowed Israel to retain control over infrastructure services such as electricity, gas, fuel, and telecommunications.

Palestinian merchants, however, were to be allowed to move freely in Israel in order to buy and sell merchandise. And work in Israel for more than 100,000 Palestinian workers was to become a major source of income for Palestine. The advantage for Israel would be that the Palestinians would return home every night, eliminating the danger of their remaining for long periods inside Israel proper, as do foreign workers from other parts of the world. Another boon to Israel was that, although the PA was not prevented from imposing protective tariffs, the Palestinian market soon became a most convenient one for Israel's industrial products. In many cases, having Palestinian markets nearby enabled Israelis to reach economies of scale that made it possible for them to sell their products elsewhere, in places where they had not previously been competitive.

The Paris agreement also provided many short-term advantages to the Palestinians. The money earned by Palestinians working in Israel, as well as the customs and excise duties collected for the PA by the better-organized Israeli tax authorities, became the PA's most stable sources of cash. And although it is difficult to assess the exact influence of the agreement on the Palestinian economy, the years immediately preceding and following its implementation were by far its best. The GNP rose, as did the standard of living, and capital began to flow into Palestine from both charitable and economic sources.

The basic flaws of the Paris agreement soon became apparent, however. Conceived at the high point of globalization, the thinking behind the agreement owed much to the visionary theories of Shimon Peres, Israel's veteran statesman. In his New Middle East doctrine, Peres envisioned that Israel would help lift all Middle Eastern countries out of their misery by providing them with technology and helping them obtain financing from the world community. Peres also hoped that the special relations he had built with King Hassan of Morocco and with some Persian Gulf states would enable Israel and the Palestinians to get involved in regional development projects.

Peres' theory, however, was naive and did not foresee some of the destructive side effects of globalization. In the case of Palestine, he overlooked the deep gaps in development and the standard of living between Israelis and Arabs. If such a gap is too great, economic association soon becomes exploitation—even with the best intentions. This lesson had been learned the hard way in the European Union, where it was found that if the gap between a new member and other EU nations was too wide, the association would not succeed. The weaker country must maintain its own economic independence until all sides can be sure that union will not eviscerate the economic institutions of the weaker country.

Even before the Paris agreement was signed in 1994, economists had begun to warn that a real economic dialogue between the two sides could become a reality only if the gap between their annual per capita GNPs—which, at that time, was $14,000 in Israel and only $2,000 in the West Bank and $800 in Gaza—was drastically narrowed. Politicians, unfortunately, ignored this warning.

The danger posed by this failure was nowhere more obvious than in employment. Since many Palestinians still live off the land and are not part of the area's labor force looking for work, long-term employment of 100,000 Palestinians in Israel would deprive Palestine of much of its major natural resource—a resource that should have been absorbed by it own industry instead. The longer the Paris agreement remained in force, the deeper economic integration between the two sides became, mostly to the detriment of the Palestinians. The benefits both sides had derived from their many years of separation were soon forgotten.

Starting in 1936, as a result of the Arab boycott and the efforts of local Jews to establish their own institutions, each community had become quite independent economically. The Jews learned to grow their own food and establish industries and infrastructure, and the Palestinians—despite having to bear the burden of 20 years of Jordanian occupation and of the refugee camps established after 1948—also established an independent economy. After the war of 1967, when Israel occupied the West Bank and Gaza, most of the economic barriers between the two communities collapsed. What few roadblocks remained were dismantled by the Paris agreement that followed Oslo, and the Palestinian economy became even more dependent on Israel's.

To be fair, the Paris agreement never had much of an opportunity to work the way it was intended to. As Ephraim Kleiman, a professor of economics at Hebrew University and an adviser to the Israeli negotiating team points out, the series of closures Israel began to impose on the Palestinians in 1995 in response to the growing wave of Palestinian terror limited economic contact and may have further contributed to the Palestinian economic slowdown that began that year. Independence now may make it much easier for Palestine to mobilize investments, loans, and know-how from foreign sources—especially from the oil-rich Persian Gulf Arab states. It will also force the Palestinians to figure out how to increase domestic entrepreneurship. Independence may even, in the future, allow Palestine to negotiate an economic cooperation agreement with Israel under much better terms than the 1994 Paris agreement.

A Last Resort

The first plans for a unilateral physical separation between areas settled by Jews and Arabs were actually made long before the beginning of the second intifada in October 2000. Contrary to what many people outside Palestine remember, the seven years after the signing of the Oslo agreement in September 1993 were not quiet at all, but marked by constant Palestinian terrorism. The subject of a fence thus began to be raised by the Israeli government as early as March 1995, when a suicide bomber killed 21 Israeli soldiers at a bus stop near Netanya. The goal of the fence was to make various closures more effective and to drastically limit the entry of Palestinians into Israel.

Discussion of the fence began in earnest in 1996, when it was raised by the minister of internal security at the time, Moshe Shahal (a member of the then ruling Labor Party). Shahal suggested the construction of a 300-mile, electronically controlled barrier with seven or eight crossing points. Although security and police experts supported his plan, it was soon shelved by Shahal's superiors. The governments of Prime Minister Yitzhak Rabin and, even more so, of Shimon Peres (who succeeded Rabin after his assassination in November 1995) were not yet ready to give up on the dream of "a New Middle East," in which the emphasis was placed on integration, not separation. Meretz, Israel's leftist party, also balked at unilateral separation, arguing that direct negotiation was the only way to solve the conflict.

The Rabin and Peres governments also held an attitude toward Arab terrorism quite different from that of their successors. Both prime ministers refused to let violence deter progress toward peace and stuck to the slogan "We must fight terror as if there are no hopes for peace and we must strive for peace as if there is no terror." The outbreak of the second intifada and the intensification of Palestinian violence has since greatly diminished the popularity of these slogans. It is worth noting, however, that when Mitzna was elected chairman of the Labor Party in November 2002, he adopted essentially the same position, rewording it as "We shall fight terror as if there are no negotiations and we shall negotiate as if there is no terror." He added, however, that if it becomes clear that negotiations are not possible, Israel should resort to unilateral separation.

When Sharon became prime minister, succeeding Ehud Barak in early 2001, he advocated a policy very different from Labor's: no negotiations without a total cessation of violence first. "We cannot be expected to negotiate under fire," Sharon said. Although this policy won the support of the Bush administration, its fatal flaw soon became obvious: it gives a veto power to the most extreme among the Palestinian terror groups. Under Sharon's policy, a single act of violence perpetrated by a marginal group can block peace talks for an unlimited period. It was thus subsequently decided to limit the condition of an "obligatory cease fire" to two weeks, and then to a week.

These modifications, however, have been to no avail. Indeed, after two years of extreme violence between Jews and Arabs, it has become obvious to both sides that a total separation, a "cooling off" period, is urgently needed. This is precisely what a fence would provide. Moreover, total physical separation may actually enable more effective international mediation that could eventually lead to a final peace agreement between Israel and the Palestinians. Although Palestinian terrorist incursions into Israel may still take place even after separation, their number and effectiveness can be expected to be much more limited.

Meanwhile, after every suicide bombing over the last few months, the voices within Israel calling to speed up the fence's construction have grown louder. Not only has the president of Israel, Moshe Katzav, expressed his support, but even Binyamin Netanyahu, Sharon's rival in the Likud Party, has demanded that all available resources be diverted to building the barrier. Mitzna and the Labor Party even made it one of their major issues in the run-up to the general elections on January 28. Accusing Sharon of dragging his feet, Mitzna admitted that completion of the first stage of the fence—now scheduled for later this year—would probably not solve all of Israel's security problems. For one thing, the fence will be short: only 100 miles, a third of the total length of the Israeli-Palestinian border. Determined suicide bombers may still be able to get across. Even before the first segment is completed, therefore, there may be a decision to extend it. Yet the fence around the Gaza Strip, which has existed for several years, has already proven valuable. No suicide bomber has come from Gaza since its completion, and in November 2002, Gazan suicide bombers headed for Israel were forced to try to get there by sea, where they were intercepted and sunk by the Israeli navy.

The completion of the first segment of the entire West Bank fence, which will run from Beit She'an to Arad, should not only provide greater security but also have other, equally important positive effects. It should convince both sides that a two-state solution has become the only viable option, and that they should stop their often violent efforts to sabotage such a resolution. Complete separation will reduce Israel's dependence on Palestinian workers and Palestinian dependence on employment in Israel. Of course, this may hurt the two states in the short term, since both sides have become dependent on each other despite the violence. The Palestinians may be the bigger losers, but some economists believe that in the long run, even they will profit from separation by becoming more self-sufficient.

Psychologically, separation will provide both sides with breathing space for several years during which, free from the pressure of ongoing violence, fundamental problems such as the equitable division of land and water and the nature of future economic and social relations can be dealt with. Issues that until recently seemed the main sticking points, such as borders, Jerusalem, and the right of return for the Arab refugees of 1948, may prove easier to resolve once agreement is reached on more fundamental topics.

Israelis who remain opposed to the fence can be divided into two groups: those who do not believe in a two-state solution and would like to "uproot" Palestinian terror through military action, and those who would like to see a separation from the Palestinians but believe that the Israeli settlements are an irreversible factor that will make a fence impractical. This latter camp would like to see a negotiated settlement leading to an "equitable solution" to the settlement question: namely, an evacuation of the outlying settlements in return for the extension of the Israeli border to include settlements in the Ariel area and in Gush Etzion.

Supporters of the fence, meanwhile, also fall into two groups. The first believes that an internal Israeli clash over the future of the settlements is coming and will occur when the fence is completed. This group, moreover, is convinced the fence will not be able to keep out suicide bombers if large numbers of Jewish settlers continue to cross it every day on their way to work inside Israel. Thus the retired general Dan Rothschild, who for many years was the coordinator of Israel's activities in the West Bank, now leads the growing pro-fence movement but believes that if Israeli guards are forced to screen 30,000 Israeli vehicles a day (the current level of Jewish traffic in and out of the territories), they will have little chance of keeping out terrorists. Most of the settlements, he argues, will therefore have to be disbanded.

Another group of Israelis, somewhat more optimistically, believes that separation may induce large numbers of settlers, especially those in isolated settlements, to give up their homes voluntarily. A survey completed in October 2002 revealed that in the preceding year, more than 20,000 settlers had returned to Israel as a result of economic and security considerations. Supporters of voluntary separation believe that generous compensation, possibly supported by outside sources, could speed up this departure of the settlers. Such a process will be difficult and in many cases heartbreaking, yet it remains imperative for the future of Jews and Arabs in Palestine.

Because unilateral separation will, one hopes, be temporary, the borders set by the fence can be adjusted when a final agreement between Israel and Palestine is reached. This will be especially necessary where the fence splits villages in two and if it is agreed that certain Israeli settlements that now fall east of the demarcation line should be included within Israel.

Not all aspects of separation should be temporary, however. No one expects that the daily influx of tens of thousands of Palestinian workers into Israel will be renewed, and much of the economic separation will remain. Many Israelis have already started to argue as much, noting the positive experiences of Israel prior to 1967. The Palestinian market does not consume many of the mostly sophisticated products Israeli industry now produces, and, like so many developed countries trying to limit the entry of foreign labor, Israel would be better off without dependence on Palestinian workers.

For its part, the Palestinian economy, already in ruins after more than two years of a devastating war with Israel, can be expected to suffer more. Despite its reservoir of semi-skilled workers, the Palestinian economy needs Israel—its ports, infrastructure, and technical assistance—as a bridge to markets in the West. Arab markets, including those of the oil-rich Persian Gulf states, offer little promise to the economy or workers of Palestine. And hopes that Palestine would become the "Singapore of the Middle East" now seem like pipe dreams amid the grim reality of 2003.

Some Israeli economists, however, such as Zvi Sussman, former deputy governor of the Bank of Israel, are more optimistic. They believe separation will be a blessing in disguise for the Palestinian economy. Sussman says that the Palestinians "need a period in which their economy will learn to fend for itself, with international help, of course." To this end, he has even urged the Palestinians to strive for their own independent currency.

Even the Israeli economy will need time to adjust to separation and to being deprived of cheap labor. Israel will have to learn to import rather than produce labor-intensive crops such as tomatoes, cucumbers, and melons. Still, Israeli entrepreneurs hope to establish workshops and factories in Palestine, similar to those they have already established in Jordan and Egypt, where Israelis mostly handle the design, engineering, and marketing, and local workers supply the labor. It can therefore be expected that some interrelationship will develop between the Israeli and Palestinian economies. Hopefully, these links will develop gradually—as the idea of two states for two peoples takes hold and clears the way for a real peace.

In sum, then, even as de facto or unilateral separation achieves concrete gains, it will also help both sides rid themselves of the ghosts of the past. In 1999, the Palestinians turned down the peace plan proposed by President Bill Clinton because it did not address the issue of Palestinian refugees of the 1948 war. Of course, the idea of allowing any number of them to return to Israel proper is a nonstarter for Israelis, whether on the right or on the left, who fear that their state would be flooded by Arabs. In future peace negotiations, after separation has become a fact, Palestinians may be prepared to address this subject in more realistic terms.

Apart from relatively small groups of Palestinians who believe in "total victory" and Israelis who claim that Palestinian terror can be "uprooted," Israelis, Arabs, and the world at large have already come to accept that there can be no military solution to the bloodshed in Palestine. That recognition alone, however, has not been sufficient to achieve real peace. The experience of the bitter conflict shows that peace can be achieved only in two stages—the first of which should be separation between the two sides, unilateral if necessary.

The Future of Palestine

Khalil Shikaki

Stateless in Gaza

Since July 2004, the Palestinian Authority (PA) has faced its most serious internal challenge since it was established in 1994. A violent showdown in the Gaza Strip between competing nationalist factions—an "old guard" and a "young guard"—has threatened to destroy the PA and, with it, what little remains of domestic security and order after four years of uprising against Israel. The ongoing turmoil represents a critical danger, not just for Palestinian society and its dreams of a unified state, but also for Israel's plan to disengage unilaterally from Gaza—a plan the United States is counting on to revive the peace process and to regain much-needed credibility in the Middle East.

If Israel implements Prime Minister Ariel Sharon's plan to withdraw from the Gaza Strip in the last quarter of 2005, Palestinian society will fragment even more, lose the benefit of unified representation, and very possibly lapse into bloody infighting. The Israelis will not get the security they want and will be forced to confront a Hamas empowered by the PA's collapse. Meanwhile, the Quartet—the United States, the UN, the European Union, and Russia—will find not only its "road map" to peace in tatters, but also that peacemaking is impossible without a strong, integrated Palestinian leadership. Continued Palestinian disarray thus affects all parties involved in the conflict. But it is not too late to change course: holding Palestinian national elections before Israel's withdrawal could

KHALIL SHIKAKI is Director of the Palestinian Center for Policy and Survey Research in Ramallah.

prevent the chaos and help establish the foundations for a democratic Palestinian state committed to peaceful relations with Israel.

Generation Gap

Sharon's withdrawal plan has exacerbated long-rising tensions within the Palestinian political community. When the al Aqsa intifada erupted in September 2000, it triggered dramatic changes in the Palestinian social and political environment. Weakened by Israeli retaliations and plagued by corruption and inefficiency, the PA speedily lost legitimacy at home and abroad. With this slide in popularity came serious internal divisions within the nationalist camp, the PA's core; the resulting power vacuum opened the way for lawlessness and a rise in the authority of Hamas and other Islamists. Not only did paralysis at the top levels of decision-making plague Palestinian government, but it also blunted Palestinian efforts to build a state or make peace.

Capitalizing on Palestinians' growing fear and thirst for revenge, Islamist groups such as Hamas and the Palestinian Islamic Jihad (PIJ) gained public favor with suicide bombings and violence against Israelis. Average Palestinians were feeling more and more threatened by Israeli-imposed checkpoints, curfews, and sieges of Palestinian cities and towns; by the separation barrier being built deep in the West Bank; and by continued Israeli land confiscation and settlement construction. Public support for the Islamists shot up from 17 percent in mid-2000—just before the intifada began—to 35 percent in mid-2004.[11] During the same period, support for Yasir Arafat's nationalist Fatah party, which dominates the PA, dropped from 37 percent to 28 percent. In the Gaza Strip, the gap between the two groups widened even more.

---

1 Figures cited here are based on multiple surveys conducted by the Palestinian Center for Policy and Survey Research (PCPSR) in Ramallah and supervised by the author. The surveys were conducted using face-to-face interviews in the West Bank and the Gaza Strip, including Arab East Jerusalem. The average sample size of each survey was about 1,320 adults. Details about the survey methodology are available at the PCPSR Web site (http://www.pcpsr.org).

Like the Islamists, Fatah's young guard used the al Aqsa intifada to undermine the prevailing Palestinian political system as much as to undermine Israeli security. By emulating Hezbollah's methods, the young militants wanted to force Israel to withdraw unilaterally from the occupied territories as it had from southern Lebanon in May 2000. But resorting to violence against the Israelis also brought the young nationalists popular legitimacy, free rein to carry arms and form militias, and a chance to intensify their fight against the old guard. Meanwhile, the escalating attacks on Israel reduced the old guard's maneuvering room in its diplomatic contacts with Israel and the international community, further damaging the PA's credibility. To improve their position vis-à-vis their older rivals, young guard militants also sought an alliance with the Islamists, while siding with refugees and the inner-city poor against the wealthy and the urban commercial class. Empowering these disenfranchised groups helped sustain the intifada despite the tremendous costs the uprising exacted on the Palestinian middle class. As long as the intifada continued, the young guard grew stronger.

At the same time, popular support for Arafat and his old guard steadily declined. Arafat's lack of vision led many Palestinians to question his judgment and leadership. His popularity decreased from 47 percent before the intifada to 35 percent by the end of its third year. In late 2003 and 2004, his popularity rating occasionally hit about 50 percent, but only in response to Israeli threats to kill or expel him. Arafat's loss of control over the treasury—the result of increased scrutiny of PA finances by the international community—made it difficult for him to use money to secure his position. Those among the armed young guard who remained loyal to him began to grumble when he was unable to pay them regular salaries.

The Palestinian public became painfully aware of the widespread corruption in the PA and its security services and grew more frustrated than ever. A survey conducted in June 2004, one month before the eruption of the Gaza turmoil, found that

87 percent of Palestinians in the occupied territories believed corruption existed in the PA. Two-thirds felt that public officials involved in, or accused of, corruption often were not charged or brought to account for their actions. Some 92 percent backed internal and external calls for fundamental political reform of the PA— the highest level ever—whereas only 40 percent believed the PA was actually carrying out any such reforms.

Sharon announced the withdrawal plan in April 2004, and since then Gaza's power brokers have predictably sought to increase their influence. For the nationalist young guard in particular, the impending Israeli disengagement means new opportunities—and fresh anxieties. On the one hand, young guard members believe they will be in an excellent position after a withdrawal; after all, their guns and bombs, not the negotiating tactics of the old guard, will be credited for the Israeli pullout. On the other hand, if Israel leaves Gaza, so will the young guard's justification for the arms and independent militias, such as al Aqsa Martyrs Brigades, that weaken the old guard's grip on the Palestinian national movement. If the young nationalists fail to topple their rivals, they will likely continue along the path of armed confrontation with Israel after the withdrawal, even if such clashes are unpopular among the Palestinian people themselves.

For its part, the old guard has not been able to quash challenges to its authority. Because Israel is withdrawing unilaterally, PA leaders are no longer needed to negotiate the end of Israeli occupation. Their increasing irrelevance, combined with public enthusiasm for clean government, has emboldened the young guard leadership, militant and moderate alike, to stand up to Arafat directly. Not since 1983, when Palestinian fighters in Syria and Lebanon rebelled against him, has Arafat faced such a critical threat to his power.

Stuck in a Rut

Since the al Aqsa intifada began more than four years ago, there have been three serious attempts at democratic reform within the PA. The first attempt, in May and June 2002, was triggered by the

Israeli reoccupation of Palestinian cities in the West Bank. The second happened in conjunction with the release of the Quartet's road map in early 2003, and the third took place during the tenure of Mahmoud Abbas as the first Palestinian prime minister, from March to September 2003. Although several important reform measures were implemented at these times, the process repeatedly stalled. One thing did change for the better, however: having tasted reform, the Palestinian people became hungry for more.

During the first attempt at reform, in May 2002, it initially seemed as if internal and external forces would align to compel Arafat to take real action. The failure of PA institutions to deliver basic services to Palestinians during Israel's reoccupation provoked overwhelming public demand for immediate change. This assertion, coupled with intense pressure from the Palestinian Legislative Council (PLC) and the Fatah Revolutionary Council, led to the creation of a detailed reform program that received almost unanimous Palestinian public support. The international community added its own wish list, and Arafat grudgingly conceded: he approved some constitutional and institutional reforms, and he set a date for national elections.

But in June 2002, the Bush administration shifted its policy closer to the position of Israel's right-wing government: linking PA regime change with progress in ending the Israeli occupation, Washington demanded Arafat's removal. Encouraged by this development, Israel imposed a siege on Arafat's headquarters in Ramallah. Instead of weakening him, however, the siege only made Arafat stronger at home and more able to resist reform. The young guard grew reluctant to criticize him for fear of being linked with Israel and the United States. The internally driven and externally supported reform campaign soon lost steam. Instead of strengthening Palestinian moderates, the Bush administration's insistence on PA regime change stung them like a slap in the face.

Nonetheless, some limited but important constitutional and institutional changes were achieved. After refusing to do so for several years, in May 2002, Arafat finally signed the Palestinian Basic

Law (a temporary constitution) and the Law of the Judiciary. The appointment of a reformist finance minister, Salam Fayyad, led to quick and substantial progress in taking PA expenditures and revenues away from Arafat and placing them under the control of the Ministry of Finance. But reforms in public security and the judiciary were short-lived and cosmetic. Israel adamantly refused to consider withdrawing its forces from Palestinian cities, handing the old guard a good excuse to shelve national elections.

After a six-month lull, the Palestinian reform movement gained new impetus when the Quartet issued its road map calling for the creation of a Palestinian prime minister—a post reformers had long wanted but that Arafat had repeatedly rejected. In February 2003, after a concerted effort by Quartet members, he finally conceded. A month later, an overwhelming majority of the plc approved the creation of the new office, giving it most of the president's powers—including those related to public finance, civil service, law and order, and internal security. Soon after, Abbas (also known as Abu Mazen)—a senior member of the old guard and an Arafat associate—received a parliamentary vote of confidence, supported by members of both the old guard and the young.

The Abbas government made serious efforts to institutionalize the reform process. Security courts, operated outside the legal system and not subject to judicial appeal, were abolished and a Supreme Judicial Council was appointed in accordance with the Judiciary Law. Several PA agencies that nominally reported to Arafat but were effectively accountable to no one were brought under government responsibility. And public finance witnessed major improvements, such as better control over public investments and the salaries of some security services.

But ultimately these reforms fell short. The idea behind the Quartet road map was that a powerful Palestinian prime minister would restore credibility to the PA leadership, which would, in turn, spur reform, reduce violence, and jump-start Israeli-Palestinian peace negotiations. When Abbas was first appointed in March, 61 percent of the Palestinian public backed him. The people expected him to deliver what Arafat could not: political reform, economic progress, an end to corruption, a return to negotiations with Israel, and the enforcement of security and a cease-fire.

Yet Arafat found ways to undermine the new prime minister's authority, effectively depriving him of his constitutional powers. Additionally, Israel did little to enhance Abbas' credibility. It failed to redeploy significantly from Palestinian territory, denied Arafat his freedom of mobility, and refused to freeze settlement construction. As a result, Abbas failed to improve the Palestinians' political or economic prospects. Very soon, he lost much of the public's confidence. After a few months, in September 2003, he was forced to resign. With Abbas went, for a time, the push for reform.

If an opportunity was missed when the Abbas government collapsed, the circumstances that led to his ascendancy revealed a significant change in the attitudes of the Palestinian public. Demand for fundamental political reform became an established fact, and more important, for the first time since the start of the al Aqsa intifada, this demand was identified with support for the peace process. In other words, those who backed the road map and opposed violence against Israeli civilians also tended to embrace a parliamentary government with the prime minister wielding power and a largely symbolic president's office. Even more intriguing, surveys from mid-2003 showed that young guard leaders and their constituents were willing to support Abbas, a leader from the old guard. Had he led the Palestinians to stable security conditions, to political reform and national elections, and to a state—even one with provisional borders—the young guard would have abandoned its arms and, most important, its temporary ally, the Islamists.

Fourth and Long

Long considered a champion of Israeli settlements in the occupied territories, Sharon now emphasizes the long-term strategic and security benefits of unilateral Israeli disengagement from the Gaza Strip—where about 7,000 heavily guarded settlers live surrounded by 1.3 million Palestinians. But for both Palestinian militants and the general public, the plan represents a victory for the armed intifada. The Islamists and the young guard, the leaders of the violent struggle, take all the credit for what they call a complete success.

But most Palestinians also recognize that the pullout could cause major problems. The emergence of a separate national entity in the Gaza Strip after Israel's disengagement would threaten the unity of a Palestinian state and its society. Such a breakup would heighten tensions among the various Palestinian political factions, causing further fragmentation in the PA, and perhaps even its eventual demise. The result would be the emergence of more radical groups, with no moderating force to counterbalance them.

In March 2004, soon after the plan's announcement, a survey found that three-quarters of Palestinians welcomed Sharon's disengagement plan, while two-thirds viewed it as a victory for the intifada. But by June, the public had grown concerned about the plan's implications: 59 percent worried about Palestinian infighting after Israel's withdrawal; only 30 percent believed the PA had a high capacity to control internal matters following the pullout; and just 31 percent thought life in Gaza would fully resume in an orderly manner once Israel left. More people feared that the withdrawal from Gaza would not be complete and that the small strip of land would become a suffocating ghetto, without access to the rest of the world. Only a third of Palestinians welcomed Israeli disengagement.

Yet the potential for change represented by the withdrawal breathed new life into the ailing Palestinian reform movement, reviving opposition to Arafat and the old guard. In the Gaza Strip, warlords, small bands of armed men, and members of the young guard began to challenge the PA openly, brandishing their weapons in public. Not all of those calling for reform did so through force; in fact, the call came from a broad social cross- section: armed and unarmed street demonstrators, militant and moderate young guard leaders and warlords, coalitions of political parties and factions, leaders of civil society and nongovernmental organizations, and senior bureaucrats and government officials, including the PLC and the current prime minister, Ahmed Qurei.

A parliamentary committee investigating the lawlessness in the Palestinian areas declared what everybody knew: Arafat was blocking reform and did not want to embark on any serious initiative to address the PA's ills. Ultimately, Arafat admitted to making some governing mistakes and said he would concede some of his security powers (which he has since failed to do). He also called for national elections in the coming year and instated a voter registration period.

But although July's unrest in Gaza never aimed at removing Arafat from power, it is highly doubtful that the concessions he has offered will satisfy the young guard, which will insist on removing many of Arafat's loyalists from power. Elections would accomplish this, but the young nationalists—all too familiar with Arafat's pattern of opportunism and scheming—do not believe he will hold them and are prepared to use violence instead. The young guard does have the weapons and the soldiers to end Arafat's, and the PA's, hold on Gaza. If the young nationalists took Gaza by force, they would probably rule with a coalition of Islamists. Even if successful, however, the young guard itself remains divided and leaderless, with little clue as to how to make peace or build a state.

Sharon has refused to negotiate his disengagement plan with Arafat's PA, preferring to implement it unilaterally. But if the withdrawal is not coordinated with a Palestinian counterpart, the pullout will almost certainly be partial and attacks against Israel will most likely continue. Palestinian power struggles will intensify and the PA will crumble, with warlords and Islamists coexisting within vaguely specified domains. Gaza will become a breeding ground for radicalism of the worst kind—leading Israel to directly reoccupy the strip with no future exit plan.

In an attempt to avert this scenario, some Israeli politicians have hinted that young guard leaders, such as Mohammad Dahlan, may become their favored liaisons to the Palestinian people. Yet although Dahlan and others command widespread support among young Fatah members in the Gaza Strip, they lack stature, credibility, and legitimacy at the national level. True, Dahlan has reached out to reformist factions of Fatah in the West Bank, forming a partnership with Marwan Barghouti, the most famous young guard leader. But the latter, jailed by Israel for life, is unlikely to back Dahlan in defiance of Arafat.

This dearth of popular, nationwide support will make it impossible for Dahlan and other young guard Gazans to negotiate legitimately with Israel or to deliver on promises of post-disengagement security and stability, unless they form an alliance with Hamas and other Islamists. Not surprisingly, Hamas views the disengagement plan as its own victory, earned by the blood of its fighters, but it may be willing to discuss an agreement: its declared motto, "partners in blood, partners in decision-making," indicates an eagerness to share power with the nationalists, and a pact with the young guard holds more potential for Hamas than a partnership with Arafat, who is unlikely ever to share genuine power.

If Israel chooses to deal with such an alliance between young nationalists and Islamists—and it may have no choice—it may gain some quiet temporarily, but this will not be sustainable. Israel, which will continue to occupy most of the West Bank and all of Arab East Jerusalem, will eventually face a much stronger foe across the Gaza border, and violence—both in the Jewish state and in the Palestinian territories—will return. In addition to increased terrorist activity, the Islamists will grow stronger and will test the nationalists at the first opportunity. Such infighting could signal the beginning of civil war between the young guard, the old guard, and the Islamists. The groups would use violence against Israel as a legitimating tool, and cast Gaza-only elections—the one chance for calm—as a betrayal of the Palestinians' larger goal of forging a state in all of the occupied territories.

At this point, Palestinians do not have many options. Arafat and the old guard have failed to reform the political system and implement their security obligations, and they are not trusted by Israel or the United States. The young guard and the Islamists will not give up the arms that gained them prominence, moreover, unless they are given a viable political alternative to force. But so far, genuine political change has been forsaken in favor of stopgap deals that avoid restructuring the PA. If this pattern continues, an independent Gaza Strip will be condemned to violence and intensified conflict with Israel. Palestinians and Israelis—not to mention the United States' already flagging credibility in the region—will suffer.

Elective Surgery

Only holding national elections now, before the Israeli withdrawal from Gaza, can help Palestinians and Israelis prevent this impending disaster. The road map, which all the relevant parties accept, calls for such elections. And by facilitating them, the United States and the rest of the Quartet can foster a stable, democratic Palestine, in addition to more peaceful Israeli-Palestinian relations. Of course, there is no guaranteed solution to the problems facing Palestinians as they anticipate their first chance at true self-rule, even if only on a small scale. But elections, if conducted honestly and efficiently, promise the best chance to end the anarchy and paralysis that afflict the Palestinian political system.

Holding elections in the Palestinian territories occupied in 1967 will achieve three principal objectives. First, it will restore the PA's legitimacy with the Palestinian people, allowing the government to take political risks for the sake of national security. The PA's comprehensive crackdown on Islamist militants in March 1996 could not have taken place had the Palestinian leadership not been validated two months earlier by the first national elections. Second, elections will begin to phase out the old guard peacefully. Even if—or more accurately, when—Arafat is reelected as president, his power will be significantly constrained. This opening will provide Hamas and the young guard with the opportunity to capitalize on the popularity they gained during the intifada and translate it into parliamentary seats. With these forces integrated into the political system, the new PA will finally have the strength to crack down on vigilante violence and collect illegal arms.

Finally, elections will institutionalize the principles of democracy, accountability, and good governance in the Palestinian political system. Elections should be based on the March 2003 constitutional amendments that shifted authority from the president to the cabinet and the prime minister. After the elections strip the old guard of much of its power, Arafat and his cohort will no longer be able to resist these fundamental changes. The Palestinian middle class, devastated during the intifada, will gain influence and counterbalance the government's authority. No single leader will again possess the absolute, concentrated power that Arafat now commands.

Polls show that elections, if held today, would result in a PLC dominated by three forces. Mainstream Fatah nationalists would win up to 40 percent of the seats (they hold 75 percent today); Hamas and the PIJ, which did not participate in the previous Palestinian elections in 1996, would earn, at most, a third of the votes; and independent nationalists and moderate Islamists would pull in more than a quarter of the ballots. The elections would also allow the Fatah young guard to wrest control of the party and the PA from the old guard peacefully and legitimately. No longer needing weapons or attacks on Israel to bolster their status, the young nationalists would be willing to disarm.

The mainstream nationalists, composed mostly of the young guard, would form the government and appoint the prime minister, but they would have to partner with independent nationalists and moderate Islamists. Although Hamas and the PIJ would almost certainly refuse to join the new government for fear of being forced to consent officially to agreements with Israel, they would still have to abide by PA decisions, even as part of the parliamentary opposition. Regardless, having won their battle against the old guard, young nationalists would lose the incentive to foster closer relations with Islamist extremists. Instead, the young guard would have to focus on co-opting or neutralizing the independents, who, by threatening to join the radical Islamists, would be able to check the power of Fatah. Arafat would be marginalized, and the new prime minister would have to worry more about his young guard colleagues, his coalition partners, and the strong parliamentary opposition than about the whims and urges of the president. In other words, the Palestinians would finally have a democracy.

For all the hope that elections offer, conditions in the West Bank and the Gaza Strip are not now conducive to holding them. On a very basic level, the ongoing violence would make it difficult for voters to reach the ballot box. Palestinian factions must thus reach an understanding on a complete cease-fire during the election period. Perhaps harder to cure, however, is the inherent distrust that the public holds for the government. Although surveys indicate that 95 percent of Palestinians want national elections, many people failed to register to vote when the process began in September 2004. There are many possible explanations for this poor initial turnout—voters waiting until the last minute to register, for example—but one thing is certain: most Palestinians have little faith in the political process. Arafat has promised elections in the past—as he does now—only to postpone them time and again. Why would he now agree to something that would limit his power?

It is true that Arafat and the older nationalists in Fatah stand to lose the most—by ceding control to both the young guard and the Islamists. But Arafat also stands to gain domestic and international legitimacy from the elections, even if his real authority is constrained. This might not be enough to force his hand, considering that he could also be deprived of a loyal majority in the PLC. But the United States and Israel could compel Arafat to give in to the reformists' demands. By removing the obstacles he has used to postpone elections in the past-checkpoints and sieges that inhibit Palestinian movement, for example—and reversing their own opposition to elections, the United States and Israel would leave Arafat little choice in the matter. The outcry of the Palestinian public and the young guard would pressure him into acquiescing, or else risk losing what little remains of his credibility.

Even if Arafat is compelled to organize elections, many hurdles will remain. Islamist groups such as Hamas boycotted the 1996 elections, and they could do so again. Like Fatah's old guard, the Islamist militants would have to give up a lot to participate in the political system: they would have to abandon the guns and bombs that fueled the intifada—and Islamist popularity—in the first place, and a segment of their constituency may not accept a cease-fire with Israel and could even break off from the group. But Islamist leaders also know that their decision not to recognize the first Palestinian elections in 1996 was a tremendous blunder: they lost all ability to influence the national agenda for the following four years—until the intifada began. Indeed, since its establishment in 1987 and with the sole exception of 1996, Hamas has participated in all types of elections in Palestinian civil society.

In fact, Hamas seems to have already accepted the trade-off of arms and militia for parliamentary seats. Hamas is fully participating in the current debate on a revised election law and has presented papers to the Palestinian Central Election Commission. Capitalizing on popular support, Hamas stands to gain a significant number of seats in the PLC. If, on the other hand, Hamas refuses to run, it could very well lose some of its popular base and face newly empowered public institutions that will force it to disband its militia. Of course, once Hamas is a part of the PA, it must be forced to adjust to the rules of the game. True, Islamist hard-liners will be able to undermine the peace process by working within the political system—just as Israeli ultraconservatives do in their government—but they will still have to obey the PA's laws. To speed up the difficult integration process, the government will need to take several steps. First and foremost, the Palestinian security services and the PA bureaucracy will have to absorb Hamas' militia until the time comes, as part of the wider implementation of the road map, to collect all illegal arms and begin the decommissioning process. No doubt, disarming will be hard for the Islamists. But further democratic reform and municipal elections, which will allow Hamas to solidify its popular support, will sweeten the bitter pill.

Collateral Advantage

Although these elections hold obvious advantages for the Palestinian people, they will also benefit Israel and the Quartet. Israel and the United States oppose elections for fear that Arafat will be re-elected, but both nations have more to gain than to lose. A Palestinian cease-fire during elections will help the Jewish state prepare for its eventual withdrawal without seeming as if it were fleeing under fire. Most important, if Israel, the United States, and the rest of the international community truly want Palestinian democracy and a credible partner in the Middle East peace process, elections will help them get both.

Despite the militancy of almost all Palestinian factions during the intifada, elections will likely moderate Palestinian discourse on the peace process. Over the last decade, surveys of Palestinians have documented a clear trend toward moderation—such as accepting Israel's Jewish character and a Palestine limited to the occupied territories. Palestinians are more willing to compromise today than at any time since the start of the peace process in 1993. Polls also demonstrate that Palestinians who have hope for a better future—including fundamental political reform—tend to reject violence and support reconciliation with Israel; elections can help supply this kind of hope. True, the al Aqsa intifada has meant a rise in public support for radical Islamist groups such as Hamas, but polls also indicate something more surprising: although there are more supporters of Hamas today than in 2000, they are much less committed to the group's ideology; many are even open to a peace agreement that embraces a two-state solution.

Still, for elections to succeed, Israel and the international community will have to make sacrifices. Israel must respect the Palestinian cease-fire by observing a cease-fire of its own. Israel needs to remove physical impediments, such as checkpoints and its stifling military presence in populated areas, and suspend activities—settlement construction, targeted assassinations—that Palestinians view as provocative. If Israel refuses to take such steps, the demands for elections will weaken, another chance at reform will be lost, and Arafat will once again blame Israel for the Palestinians' continued misery.

The United States and other international actors must ensure that the Palestinians and Israel implement their election-related commitments. Regional and international monitors from bodies considered unbiased by the Palestinians, such as Japan, Russia, the EU, and the UN, will have to guarantee the validity of the elections—and strong political pressure will be needed to make sure they actually take place. Washington and the rest of the Quartet must also set a binding election date, as well as the length of the election period.

U.S. credibility is now so low in the Middle East that the White House will have to work behind the scenes. But as Israel's principal ally, its role will be crucial. Palestinian elections present the Bush administration with the opportunity to give concrete expression to its declared commitment to pursuing both Israeli-Palestinian peace and regional democracy. By supporting elections, and thus linking peace making to democracy building, the White House can begin to quell the suspicion pervasive among Arabs that its intervention in Middle Eastern politics is motivated solely by expediency and self-interest, rather than a sincere desire to initiate regionwide reform and good governance. Without changing this deep-seated belief, neither the United States nor its allies will ever truly defeat Islamist extremism.

Israel's New Strategy

Barry Rubin

The End of Occupation

Israeli politics and policy are undergoing a revolutionary transformation—one of the most important developments in the nation's history. As dramatic as recent events have been, equally important is the emergence of a new strategic paradigm that reverses 30 years of debate and practice and overturns some of Israelis' most basic assumptions.

Why have perceptions, politics, and strategy changed so dramatically? The shift began when Prime Minister Ariel Sharon ordered a complete withdrawal from the Gaza Strip and parts of the West Bank, including the dismantling of Jewish settlements in those areas. Within a few months, Sharon's Likud Party had revolted against him; Sharon had quit Likud and formed another party, Kadima; the Labor Party had chosen a populist outsider as its leader; the governing coalition had collapsed, necessitating new elections; Sharon had been physically incapacitated by a stroke and replaced by a top deputy, Ehud Olmert; and Olmert had gone on to win in the March 2006 elections. Hamas' victory in the January 2006 Palestinian elections only underscored already existing trends.

The emerging new policy is based on a broad Israeli recognition that holding on to the West Bank and the Gaza Strip is simply not in Israel's interest, despite the fact that the Palestinian leadership has been uninterested in and incapable of making peace and that

BARRY RUBIN is Director of the Global Research in International Affairs (GLORIA) Center, Interdisciplinary Center, and Editor of the Middle East Review of International Affairs. His latest book is *The Long War for Freedom: The Arab Struggle for Democracy in the Middle East*.

both Fatah and Hamas will use that land to try to launch attacks on Israel. The territories no longer serve a strategic function for Israel, given the unlikelihood of a conventional attack by Arab state armies, and Israel could better defend its citizens by creating a strong defensive line rather than by dispersing its forces. Moreover, because a comprehensive peace deal is not likely to be reached for many years, the territories are no longer of value as bargaining chips. During the long era before the Palestinians will be organized and moderate enough to make peace, Israel has to set its own strategy based on these realities.

Territory for Peace?

The international situation changed drastically in the 1990s, but until recently, Israel was too busy with shorter-term crises and closer-to-home issues to integrate new external realities into its thinking. The Cold War ended, the Soviet Union fell, and the United States became the world's sole superpower. In 1991, a U.S.-led coalition defeated Iraq and forced it out of Kuwait. Meanwhile, Arab states became less interested in waging the Arab-Israeli conflict; the Palestine Liberation Organization (PLO), after decades of battling Israel without achieving its goals, had reached a low point.

At first, it seemed that such changes—plus an accumulation of Palestinian defeats and internal troubles—would push Palestinian leaders, Syria, and most Arab states toward a peace agreement with Israel. The peace process was an experiment to see if this would in fact happen. In 2000, both Syria and the Palestinians (under the Clinton plan and the Camp David accords) rejected peace, proving those expectations wrong.

That result, most Israelis concluded, was not a product of some misunderstanding, U.S. or Israeli intransigence, a slight diplomatic misstep, or a need to make minor changes in the deal being offered. On the contrary, the Palestinian and Syrian leaderships were simply not ready for peace—because of radical forces and ideologies, hard-line personalities, extremist goals, and the fact that the conflict bolstered dictators who would otherwise have faced serious domestic problems. With their own hopes shattered, Israelis from across the political spectrum reluctantly accepted that the conflict would endure for a long time.

The Israeli response to this realization was defined by a historic Israeli debate over national strategy, the perceived lessons of the Oslo experience, and the Israelis' analysis of Palestinian political realities. A sector of the Israeli public had always wanted to keep the territories captured in the 1967 Six-Day War for religious or nationalist reasons, but this was always a minority position and not—except in the case of East Jerusalem—government policy. The real galvanizing arguments for retaining the territories were strategic and diplomatic: first, holding on to the West Bank and the Gaza Strip gave Israel strategic depth, which it could use to defend itself against a conventional military attack; and second, the territories could be used as bargaining chips when there was a Palestinian partner ready to make a lasting peace—"territory for peace," as the slogan went. Labor and Likud alike invoked these arguments in supporting Jewish settlements in the territories. Both parties favored holding on to the West Bank and Gaza until real progress was made on the diplomatic front.

This position was rational for several reasons. For much of Israel's history, the main strategic threat to the country was a conventional war on its borders with Arab states. In this context, it was vital to possess the West Bank, especially, in order to control the Jordan Valley and use the north-south ridges to its west as positions to defend against an attack by Iraqi, Jordanian, Saudi, or Syrian forces. Holding the territories also gave Israel a buffer against Palestinian terrorists striking from across the border, a threat magnified from irritating to existential by the fact that such forces had Arab and Soviet- bloc help. At the same time, it was assumed that those "behind" Israel's defensive lines—West Bank and Gaza Palestinians—would present only a limited security problem.

That strategic concept worked very well for 20 years—until the first intifada in the late 1980s—and reasonably well for another decade. As time wore on and many Israelis came to believe that there was a real possibility of a negotiated resolution, the "territory for peace" argument became even stronger. That notion was the basis of the 1993 Oslo agreement with the PLO. Prime Minister Yitzhak Rabin, Foreign Minister Shimon Peres, and other Israeli leaders thought that yielding territory would be the confidence-building measure that would persuade the Palestinians that Israel was ready for a deal.

The Failure of Oslo

Israel's experience with the Oslo peace process from 1993 to 2000 reshaped that strategic thinking. Believing peace was possible, Israel made big concessions and took real risks, and a majority of its leaders and people accepted the creation of a Palestinian state and withdrawal from almost all the territory captured in 1967 as tolerable compromises for peace. Israel recognized the PLO, let its forces—including many terrorists—return from exile to the West Bank and Gaza, and gave it guns and control over territory. This policy was based on the PLO's promises that it would recognize Israel and cease incitement to destroy Israel, stop its own terrorism, and dismantle groups based in the territories that were trying to attack Israel. Even as few of these commitments were kept, many Israelis argued that all these problems would be resolved when final negotiations began and the Palestinians saw real progress toward an end to the occupation and received a state of their own and billions of dollars in compensation aid.

But the Oslo process failed—and whatever Israel's responsibility for this failure, the Israelis concluded that the main fault lay with the other side. Until 2000, many Israelis believed that if they just kept offering and giving more—if they only did a better job of implementation or showed more empathy—it would be possible to reach comprehensive peace. This yearning, along with the blistering self-criticism so typical of Israeli society, inspired much wishful thinking. In the end, however, even a majority of the left came to realize that such optimism neither accorded with the facts nor provided a basis for policy—at least not if Israel was to survive.

When, in 2000, Prime Minister Ehud Barak offered the Palestinians an independent state with its capital in East Jerusalem in exchange for full peace, the Palestinian leadership passed up the opportunity. Instead, what followed was a five-year terrorist war in which over a thousand Israelis were killed—many of them with weapons Israel had permitted the Palestinian Authority (PA) to have and by gunmen Israel had released from prison or allowed to return to the territories. Anti-Israel incitement in official PA statements and in Palestinian schools, mosques, and media urged Israel's destruction and the murder of its citizens. Israeli concessions were turned into weapons that were used to kill Israel's people—a lesson not easily disregarded. Although they would have preferred not to reach this conclusion, the overwhelming majority of Israelis came to doubt that the existing Palestinian leadership would ever be a real partner for peace.

At first, the Oslo experience appeared mainly to have subverted the position of the left in Israel, but it actually proved that both the left and the right had been wrong. The left had thought that Palestinian leader Yasir Arafat would make a deal and keep it, and the right had expected him to make a deal and break it. Advocates of the process argued that if Arafat was offered a good deal—a Palestinian state in the West Bank and Gaza, much of East Jerusalem, an end to the occupation, and a lot of compensation money—he would make peace. The resulting Palestinian state would have a stake in maintaining stability and raising its citizens' living standards; Palestinian refugees would return with billions of dollars raised abroad; Arab states would line up to make peace; and the conflict would be over. Meanwhile, the right was critical of the peace process not because it rejected peace but because it assumed that the process was a trap. It thought Arafat would take the West Bank and Gaza, make a Palestinian state, and then use that state as a springboard to try to wipe Israel off the map. With cross-border attacks, and Arab states or Iran potentially sending arms and armies, there would be no end to the conflict—and Israel's strategic position would have deteriorated.

Neither outcome came to pass. No one foresaw that Arafat would be offered the bargain the left proposed, reject it, and resort to all-out war. For the Israelis, the year 2000 was a revelation. Palestinian and Syrian leaders thought ready for peace instead chose to continue the conflict. Palestinian leaders kept the refugees' "right of return" as their highest priority, which the Israelis saw as a sign that destroying Israel was more important to Palestinian leaders than ending the occupation. The Israelis concluded that their long-standing belief in the Palestinians' desire for peace was fundamentally flawed.

From then on, the Palestinian leadership was seen as being unready—and certainly not eager—for peace. The confidence-building process had failed. Concessions had come back to bite, rather than reward, the country. How, Israelis asked, could they respond to these revelations in order to develop a new approach?

Paradigm Shift

Since the failure of the peace process in 2000, the thinking of the Israelis has been very much affected by the experience of having to defend themselves against one of the bloodiest onslaughts of terrorism in history, along with an international campaign to brand Israel a pariah state that does not deserve to exist. But other developments elsewhere also helped create a new strategic paradigm. These included the September 11, 2001, attacks on the United States, the war on terrorism, Saddam Hussein's overthrow, the rise of an Arab democracy movement challenging the status quo, Arafat's death and the lack of any strong nationalist Palestinian leader to replace him, and the rise of Hamas and other radical Islamist movements in the Arab world. Many of these events increased the underlying sense in Israel that the problem stemmed not from Israel's lack of generosity but from the nature of its adversary. Achieving peace, the Israelis concluded, would be harder and take longer than they had hoped or expected.

At the same time, a number of other developments suggested that although the conflict would continue, it would not spread or escalate. For one, Saddam's fall removed a major threat. Meanwhile, other Arab regimes—challenged by Islamists and strategically weak—started to be willing to sacrifice some of their support for the Palestinians in exchange for improved relations with the United States. Even if they would not make peace with Israel, they also did not want war, and their support for the Palestinians hit rock bottom. And all of this reinforced the trends set off by the ending of the Cold War and the consequent shift in the international balance of power. Israel's security environment started to look very different. Arab armies and arms appeared less dangerous, and occupying territory became less important than having clear defensive lines that did not enclose a hostile population.

What emerged from the shock of the failure of Oslo and the five-year-long terrorist war that followed was a new synthesis in Israeli thinking: a national consensus along centrist lines, drawing ideas from across the political spectrum. From the left came the idea that Israel should withdraw from the captured territories, dismantle many of the settlements, and accept an independent Palestinian state in exchange for real peace. This melded with the right's belief that there would be no partner with whom to make real peace for a long time to come.

These two notions fused into a new paradigm, which dominates Israeli politics and thinking today, even as the Palestinians stick to a policy that combines weakness and intransigence. Although the Israelis' most optimistic hopes have been dashed, most Israelis now believe that the situation can actually be made more secure with the right approach.

The Israeli military played a considerable role in developing this new viewpoint. Its main mission, the generals concluded, had become patrolling the West Bank and the Gaza Strip, where it protected roads and settlements while combating terrorists on terms largely set by the enemy. Not only did this stretch forces too thin, but it also sacrificed the strategic advantages Israel held.

Moreover, protecting Israeli territory and citizens was made harder by the lack of a discernible or defensible boundary. This problem could not be remedied as long as the army was required to defend every Jewish settlement and deal with a large, hostile civilian population.

The idea of a defense based on a clear line laid out along advantageous terrain was far more attractive to strategists. Dangerously exposed settlements could be evacuated, and new security fences would offer additional protection to Israeli citizens. With the protection of marine patrols off the Gaza Strip, airpower, and short-term raids into the territories, the only remaining vulnerability would be from missiles fired over the frontier, which was as much of a problem when Israeli forces were actually on the ground in the West Bank and Gaza.

The End of Wishful Thinking

Along with the military officers, both Israeli politicians and the Israeli public recognized that adopting a sustainable framework for defense would mean giving up on the idea that the PA would ever be of help in fighting terrorism; experience had taught Israel that the Palestinian leadership was at best useless and at worst a de facto ally of terrorists. In an October 2004 interview with Haaretz, Dov Weisglass, an adviser to Sharon, said that for a long time, the "assumption was that when the Palestinian majority gets national satisfaction, they will lay down their arms and the occupiers and the occupied will emerge from the trenches and embrace and kiss." But Sharon understood that no Palestinian leadership would force a moderate policy on Palestinian society and that, in the words of Weisglass, "Palestinian terrorism is in part not national at all, but religious. Therefore, granting national satisfaction will not solve the problem of this terrorism."

The consensus was that there was little chance of a deal with the Palestinians due to the nature of their politics and their leadership. Virtually no one in the Palestinian leadership had really tried to alter that nature in the 1990s, and Palestinian leaders increasingly and openly endorsed radical positions after 2000. Whatever good intentions Palestinian leader Mahmoud Abbas may have, he is too weak to impose order or to make the tough decisions necessary for peace, especially given the absence of any strong moderate faction that could help remake Palestinian politics. While in control, Arafat's Fatah movement simply did not offer such leadership, and its corruption and incompetence were destroying it (as became evident with its downfall in the January 2006 elections). Moreover, the sheer multiplicity and fractiousness of the various Palestinian factions made the imposition of order—or any coherent policy, other than the lowest-common-denominator option of simply continuing the conflict—almost impossible. And even as Fatah was overwhelmingly dominated by extremists, including both unreconstructed old hard-liners and a younger generation that glorified the terrorism of the al Aqsa Brigades, Hamas was becoming steadily more powerful.

Meanwhile, the Palestinians' desire to eliminate Israel came to seem too strong, their glorification of violence too powerful, to overcome. It seemed that Palestinian leaders would never stop inciting terrorism or arming terrorist groups. Palestinian leaders, Palestinian activists, and the general Palestinian public continued to believe that total victory, meaning Israel's destruction, was possible. Even when polls showed the existence of more moderate views among average Palestinians, these never made it into the programs of the leadership, much less onto the agendas of the gunmen who attacked Israel and sowed chaos among their own people.

This analysis is summarized in Weisglass' description of Sharon's views, which were shaped in large part by Olmert, his closest lieutenant and now his successor. Weisglass explained: "Sharon doesn't think that after a conflict of 104 years, it's possible to come up with a piece of paper that will end the matter. He thinks the other side had to undergo a deep and extended sociopolitical change." Most Israelis saw no sign that this process was even starting. On the contrary, Palestinian politics was moving in the opposite direction, as the later election of Hamas would so clearly demonstrate. With Hamas in power, Abbas now has become even more powerless, Fatah is turning more radical and violent in a desperate attempt to compete with the Islamists, and there has been an intensification of incitement of the younger Palestinian generation to continue the struggle for many years.

The Israelis hope that someday things will be different—but they are aware that that day might be very far in the future. In case it does come, however, Israel's new policy has made clear its willingness to make a real compromise peace. Meanwhile, however, Israel needed a new strategy to fit existing conditions. In Weisglass' words, "When you're playing solitaire, when there is no one sitting across from you at the table, you have no choice but to deal the cards yourself."

When Weisglass said the peace process should be put in "formaldehyde," he did not mean that Sharon sought to kill it. One does not kill something with formaldehyde; one preserves it for the future. Weisglass was saying that Israeli policy must keep open the chance for successful negotiations with the Palestinians—but that there needs to be an interim era before that could happen.

Go it Alone

This was the context in which Sharon decided on complete withdrawal from the Gaza Strip and the dismantling of several West Bank settlements. As the next step, during the 2006 election campaign, his successor, Olmert, announced a policy of "convergence," in which Israel would withdraw from most of its remaining positions in the West Bank, dismantle many more settlements, and consolidate those "settlement blocs" that it intended to claim in the future.

The idea of separation between Israel and the territories has a bipartisan history. It was first raised by former Defense Minister Yitzhak Mordechai, of the Likud, then by Barak, of Labor. Unilateral withdrawal was advocated by Labor in the 2002 elections (although voters rejected the idea, and Sharon opposed it, when it was presented as part of an effort to persuade the Palestinians of Israel's good faith rather than as part of a coherent strategic policy). In his first years in office, Sharon was also unenthusiastic about building a security fence in the West Bank. Historically, the political right in Israel opposed this project for fear that it might demonstrate Israel's readiness to give up almost all of the West Bank. On this point, as on the question of unilateral withdrawal from Gaza, Sharon would make a total turnaround.

What happened to make Sharon completely reverse himself, to the point where many of his party colleagues denounced him? Olmert claims that he first introduced the idea, which, along with the defense establishment's analysis of the factors mentioned above, spurred a major rethinking by Sharon.

Certainly, Israel had never wanted the Gaza Strip for much except defensive purposes. In 1992, at the start of talks with the PLO, Israel's opening offer included turning over the Gaza Strip to Palestinian rule. Since 1994, most of the territory had been under PA control. A decade later, the Israelis were reluctant to withdraw not because of any intrinsic desire for that territory, but because of their concern that the area would become a base for attacking Israel. Many also worried that withdrawal from Gaza would be taken as a precedent for giving up all of the West Bank and be claimed by terrorists as a victory, thereby inspiring more terrorism and undercutting Israel's efforts to bargain about anything else. These were impressive arguments, but by 2004 they no longer persuaded even a historically hard-line prime minister.

Withdrawing from the Gaza Strip was still painful for Israel's leaders and citizens. The voluntary relinquishment of territory captured in an ongoing war when an opponent refuses to make peace (or even accept its enemy's right to exist) is virtually unprecedented. To reach a democratic choice, overwhelmingly supported by Israeli public opinion, to implement this disengagement, basic assumptions needed to be reconsidered. Could Israel redeploy without seeming to make this a victory for terrorism? Was the country ready to uproot citizens who had lived in Gaza for decades? Did redeployment mean giving up an asset in the negotiating process while getting nothing from the other side? Would the territory abandoned simply become a base for more terrorist attacks on Israel?

In changing the country's strategic concept, Sharon had to answer these questions—at the risk of paying a high political price. Before announcing his withdrawal plan, he was hugely popular on both the right and the left. His Likud Party was certainly solidly behind him, and he could continue as prime minister as long as he wanted. Afterward, his party split, with half of it furious and ready to replace him; his political future was in doubt, if only temporarily.

Sharon had a number of a strong motives for taking such a great political and strategic risk. He wanted his legacy to show that he was a moderate who sought peace and left his country more secure. But he recognized Israel's need for a sustainable strategic stance as long as a comprehensive diplomatic solution remained out of reach. He came to realize that holding territory was no longer strategically advantageous (and was perhaps detrimental in a long war of attrition) and accepted the demographic reality that Israel, if it did not change its approach, would soon be ruling over an Arab population outnumbering its own Jewish population. Sharon also wanted to put the ball in the Palestinians' court by forcing them to show whether they could govern a territory that was, for most practical purposes, a state. Turning over the Gaza Strip, said Weisglass, meant there were "no more excuses. . . . The whole world is asking what they intend to do with this slice of land." In the end, Israel even turned over control of the Gazan-Egyptian border to the PA. In response to the argument that holding on to land provided a bargaining chip in negotiations, Sharon simply asked, What is the value of having bargaining chips when there is no one with whom to bargain?

Meanwhile, Sharon believed that security fences would offer a viable line to which Israeli forces could withdraw and that, having won the 2000-2005 war, Israel could redeploy its troops on its own terms—the result of a victory over terrorism rather than a defeat by it. Israel could still retaliate as needed, and alternative defensive security measures seemed promising. According to polls, about 80 percent of Israelis viewed unilateral withdrawal from Gaza and parts of the West Bank as attractive.

If Palestinian policy had been different, the withdrawal could have initiated real progress toward peace. If the Palestinian leadership had been able to maintain order, stop terrorism, and make the Gaza Strip a showcase for a moderate Palestinian state, it would have garnered support internationally and within Israel for a comprehensive settlement. Few Israelis expected this to happen, but the withdrawal was a genuine chance for the Palestinian leadership to prove such skepticism wrong. It has not.

A New Consensus

Translation of the new paradigm for Israel's strategy into action began with a move by Sharon that not only left out the Palestinians but also was made without consulting his own party. When the dust cleared, the political realignment put Labor on Sharon's left, his new Kadima Party in the center, and Likud on his right.

Those remaining in Likud, now led by former Prime Minister Binyamin Netanyahu, took the traditional stance of trying to hold on to all the remaining territory captured in 1967, agreeing that the current Palestinian movement was no partner for peace but rejecting the new paradigm intended to respond to this situation. Yet even in Likud, a large faction led by former Foreign Minister Silvan Shalom basically accepted the new Sharon-Olmert strategic concept.

Labor focused on an entirely different part of the national consensus. Since its past eagerness to make concessions was so discredited, it emphasized domestic social issues instead. At the same time, its leaders essentially accepted the new strategic paradigm, a stance that hardened after Hamas' electoral victory.

Kadima embodied the new national consensus—and thus won the March 2006 elections. The common goal of its diverse members and supporters was to prioritize the new strategic agenda: ensuring Israel's security by strengthening its defenses against terrorism, rejecting wishful thinking, and consolidating control over those relatively small portions of the West Bank that Israel intends to claim as part of a diplomatic settlement.

All of this rethinking and recasting of policy happened before Hamas won the January 2006 Palestinian elections. When the Israelis concluded there was no Palestinian partner for peace, they were thinking of Fatah and Abbas, not Hamas. The Hamas victory only reinforced this view, and also proved its accuracy to many foreign observers.

With Sharon incapacitated and Kadima's victory inevitable, Olmert's party did not do as strongly as expected in the March elections. Some voters stayed home; others cast their ballots to express support for special-interest parties. Nevertheless, those parties endorsing the new paradigm generally did well, and those of the far left or far right did very badly. Having made clear his plan before election day, Olmert could claim that he had received a mandate for it.

The basic elements of the new paradigm now constitute the program of Israel's new government and probably will for a long time. Israel wants peace. It is ready to be flexible, to take risks and make concessions, and to agree to a Palestinian state in most of the West Bank and all of the Gaza Strip. The goal is not occupation but security and the right to exist as a society not under foreign attack. At the same time, the Israelis believe that there is no partner for peace, nor will there be one anytime soon. A few scattered, ambiguously "moderate" statements by Hamas will not fool them into thinking Hamas has changed, especially as it continues inciting, facilitating, and endorsing terrorist attacks.

Olmert's "convergence" policy is the expression of these beliefs. In an April 9 interview with The Washington Post, Olmert offered a succinct summary of that policy: Settlements outside the security fence will eventually be removed and their residents "converged into the blocs of settlements that will remain under Israeli control. . . . The rest of the territories will not have any Israeli presence and will allow territorial contiguity for a future Palestinian state." Israel's goal, which it will seek on an interim basis, is to have borders fairly close to, but not precisely coinciding with, those of the pre-1967 period.

A key factor in this defensive orientation will be completion of the security fence to protect Israel from attack, but with efforts taken to minimize Palestinian suffering, including altering the fence's route in response to Palestinian suits in Israeli courts. Another vital element will be Israel's retention of the right of military action to prevent terrorist attacks, including missile firings, and to ensure that those carrying out such operations will not be able to do so in future.

Despite its critical evaluation of Palestinian politics, Israel will try to help moderate Palestinians, but it has no illusions about their strength or the extent of their pragmatism. What is important is not whether Israeli officials meet with Abbas or other Palestinian officials, but whether there is any reason to believe such discussions could have a real result.

Finally, given this new consensus on peace and security issues, the Israelis are focusing on domestic socioeconomic issues. Israel has succeeded remarkably well in building its economy and infrastructure and increasing its living standards given the great strains brought about by security needs and spending on settlements. Yet changes of recent years, many of them paralleling trends elsewhere in the world, have widened socioeconomic gaps, undercut Israel's sense of community, and kept health-care, educational, and other institutions from being better. With a new security paradigm in place and many old debates concluded, the Israelis believe the time has come to focus on such problems.

This revolution has promoted national unity. Those who think Israel can obtain peace simply by giving up more, as well as those who think Israel should keep all the territories, have been pushed to the margins of both politics and debate. Facing reality and making the best out of difficult conditions have triumphed over wishful thinking. This is the kind of approach that suits an Israeli political culture that has always focused on the art of the possible. Relative optimism, in this case, is the result of making the most of an apparently insoluble situation that would otherwise seem to engender only hopelessness.

Can Hamas Be Tamed?

Michael Herzog

The Great Experiment

Much has happened in the decade between the first parliamentary elections for the Palestinian Authority (PA), in 1996, and the second, this year. The Oslo peace process staggered forward and then collapsed; a second Palestinian intifada raged and subsided; Israel erected a barrier fence along part of the West Bank and withdrew from Gaza; and Yasir Arafat, the founder and personification of Palestinian nationalism, passed from the scene. Meanwhile, Hamas—the largest Islamist group in the Palestinian community—continued its march into the political arena. Having boycotted the first elections, it campaigned vigorously in the second, and with its stunning victory in January, now stands poised to play a major role in Palestinian governance.

Hamas' involvement in the democratic process may strike many as a profound irony. After all, the group fields a private army, embraces violence as a political tool, regularly orchestrates terrorist attacks, and is dedicated to the destruction of Israel and the establishment of an Islamist state ruling the territory of Israel and the PA. Granting Hamas legitimate political status and access to the prerogatives of state power seems to be asking for trouble.

A number of optimistic observers argue, however, that this concern is overblown. It is precisely the burdens and responsibilities

MICHAEL HERZOG is a Brigadier General in the Israel Defense Forces and a Visiting Fellow at the Washington Institute for Near East Policy. He was formerly the senior military aide to Israel's Minister of Defense and the head of strategic planning for the IDF.

that come with democratic politics, they claim, that will tame Hamas. After all, as the Carnegie Endowment's Marina Ottaway wrote last summer, "There is ample evidence that participation in an electoral process forces any party, regardless of ideology, to moderate its position if it wants to attract voters in large numbers." Once trapped in a normal political mode, these observers argue, Hamas will have to answer to a more diverse array of constituencies and either deliver practical results or risk being marginalized for failing to do so. Hamas will thus effectively be forced to sheathe its sword and behave. Instead of being concerned about Hamas' new role, the optimists contend, outsiders should actually welcome it as the most likely catalyst for moving the group's focus from radical rejectionism to mainstream politics.

The logic behind such a theoretical evolution is solid, and there are indeed examples of nondemocratic political actors making the journey to respectability through participation in routine democratic processes. The problem is that few of these examples have much in common with Hamas—and those that do are much less encouraging. For all the confident assertions that everything will be fine, comparative analysis suggests skepticism is in order about whether the conditions are ripe for Hamas to be co-opted by its political participation or if instead Hamas will simply use political participation as another vehicle for pursuing its alarming core objectives. What the political inclusion of Hamas has really started, in other words, is a momentous experiment—the results of which will have a major impact on the future of Palestine, Israel, and the Middle East at large.

From Pariah to Player

Hamas was founded in 1987 as an offshoot of the pan-Islamic Muslim Brotherhood movement. It sought to address Palestinian nationalist aspirations and grievances from an Islamic perspective; its name, which means "strength," "bravery," and "zeal" in Arabic, is also an acronym for Harakat al-Muqawama al-Islamiya, or the Islamic Resistance Movement.

The group's ideology was set forth in its 1988 covenant, which remains operative to this day. The covenant defines Palestinian nationalism and the conflict with Israel in religious terms: the land of Palestine "from the river to the sea" is considered an Islamic waqf, an "endowment," and so no Muslim has the right to cede any part of it. The covenant explicitly calls for the obliteration of the state of Israel through the power of the sword and portrays the Jews as the source of all evil in the world. Freemasons, Rotarians, and members of organizations similar to theirs are denounced as Zionist agents, and they too are threatened with obliteration. The covenant stipulates that peace between Muslims, Christians, and Jews should only be permitted "under the wing of Islam."

Soon after its founding, Hamas became a major player in both Palestinian-Israeli relations and domestic Palestinian politics, pursuing a dual agenda through the parallel development of an operational and a social wing. The former now oversees hundreds of militants devoted to armed struggle against Israel and is in the process of building a backup militia of several thousand. It has been responsible for countless acts of terror—from abductions and murders to suicide bombings and rocket attacks—which have killed hundreds of Israelis, most of them civilians. The group's social arm (dawa), meanwhile, has developed a network of charities and religious, educational, and cultural institutions, positioning Hamas as an attractive provider of social services and an alternative to the hapless and corrupt PA.

Unlike, say, the Irish Republican Army (IRA), Hamas does not have an explicit separation between its military and its political wing. All its branches answer to the same organizational authority, which makes the principal decisions on terror operations as well as on political, social, and other policies. Hamas does, however, recognize both an "internal" leadership, living inside the Palestinian territories, and an "external" one, living outside, primarily in Damascus. (The latter seems attuned less to the practical realities on the ground than to the radical environment in the region.)

Arafat believed that it was possible to pursue diplomacy with and violence against Israel simultaneously, and he wanted to avoid major conflict within the Palestinian community. As a result, he tolerated Hamas' opposition to the peace process in both word and deed as long as the group did not directly challenge Oslo's foundations or his own political authority. He tried to co-opt the movement while keeping it at arm's length.

When Arafat died in November 2004, Hamas calculated that the time had come to step forward as a political party and make a bid for legitimate political power. This decision was driven by a number of factors, including the PA's disarray following years of chaotic and corrupt leadership; the weak position of Arafat's successor as president, Mahmoud Abbas; the opportunity to claim credit for Israel's disengagement from Gaza and a share of that territory's subsequent management; and Hamas' own growing reputation as an effective social-service provider and militia.

Abbas made Hamas' decision easier, first by campaigning in the January 2005 presidential election on a platform that clearly differentiated the ruling Fatah Party's appeal from Hamas' (by emphasizing nonviolence and the PA's monopoly on arms) and then by failing to translate the broad mandate he received into serious reforms or effective governance. Sensing its moment, last March, Hamas accepted a temporary cease-fire with Israel in return for Abbas' agreement to incorporate the group into both the Palestine Liberation Organization and the PA's electoral system. Because the deal did not require Hamas to disarm or abandon violence permanently and promised the movement some formal input (through the PLO) in determining Palestinian negotiating positions on final-status issues such as the repatriation of refugees, it rewarded Hamas' violent course and eroded Abbas' own political standing. But the Palestinian leader apparently felt he had little choice, thanks to his own weakness.

It took U.S. and Israeli policymakers some time to focus their attention on this emerging challenge, and when they did, it was too late to do much about it. Although Washington has consistently

Michael Herzog

denounced Hamas' ideology and militancy, it decided not to let these concerns stand in the way of the 2006 Palestinian legislative elections. "This is going to be a Palestinian process, and I think we have to give the Palestinians some room for the evolution of their political process," noted Secretary of State Condoleezza Rice last September. Washington accepted Abbas' assertion that political participation will either transform Hamas or marginalize it.

Israeli officials also found themselves without many practical options. During a mid- September visit to Washington, Israeli Prime Minister Ariel Sharon threatened not to facilitate elections in the West Bank if Hamas participated. Under U.S. pressure, he clarified his position two months later, saying, "While we will not interfere in the elections, we will not coordinate . . . and will not allow Hamas members to either work or move about other than they do today."

From the moment Hamas entered the field, polls consistently indicated that it would earn at least a third of the vote and possibly much more in the elections. Its popularity, according to the same polls, stems less from widespread support for its extremist ideology than from dissatisfaction with the PA's corruption and the stagnant Palestinian economy. Understanding this situation well, Hamas ran on a platform stressing reform and good governance rather than ideological struggle. With such a practical appeal and (following its sweeping victory in December's municipal elections) its day-to-day responsibility for the living conditions of almost a third of the population in the territories, Hamas clearly positioned itself as a plausible, and formidable, alternative to the old PA leadership.

History Lessons

Some observers detect signs that Hamas is already evolving in a moderate direction. They point to its very willingness to engage in elections and enter the Palestinian Legislative Council, an institution born from the Oslo peace process, which the group has long rejected; its acceptance of a temporary truce (tahdiya) with Israel;

its expressed willingness to consider a longer cease-fire (hudna) should Israel withdraw to its 1967 borders; and various statements by Hamas leaders that exhibit flexibility.

There is, however, overwhelming evidence pointing in the opposite direction. For example, Mahmoud al-Zahar, the group's leading figure, gave a series of interviews in the run-up to the parliamentary elections in which he explained that the group sees no connection between the elections and the Oslo process—which is dead anyway—and that any cease-fire along the 1967 borders would not come with a recognition of Israel or relations with it, but would be merely a step in the continued struggle. "Some Israelis think that when we talk of the West Bank and Gaza it means we have given up our historic war," Zahar told an Israeli newspaper in late October. "This is not the case." As for Hamas' stance on democracy, Zahar's words have been equally discouraging: he proclaimed, "We will join the Legislative Council with our weapons in our hands," later adding, "In the Islamist Palestinian state, every citizen will be required to act in accordance with the codes of Islamic religious law"—not exactly a Western vision of how democracy should function.

The debate over what to expect from Hamas has often drawn on supposed lessons of history. Optimists point to several cases in which illiberal movements or groups conformed to liberal norms once ensconced in democratic political systems. Such was the case with many European socialist parties after World War I and with erstwhile communist parties in many eastern European and former Soviet countries more recently. In recent decades, several political groups in Latin America on both the right and the left have managed to move past their antidemocratic and even violent histories to become normal political actors. Rice herself has cited Ireland and Angola as examples of countries in which unsavory forces have opted for ballots over bullets. Pessimists, in contrast, note that the Nazis initially played by the rules of Weimar Germany's democratic system and rode electoral success to power, only to turn around and establish a tyranny. The Italian fascists did the same.

A more useful analogy can be found in the modern history of the Muslim Middle East, with its assortment of relatively young independent states—nations where there is no democratic tradition or culture and where the governments have been challenged by Islamist movements advocating for the imposition of sharia while brandishing swords. In Turkey, the Islamists have been co-opted successfully, to the extent that the leader of the Islamist Justice and Development Party (AKP), Recep Tayyip Erdogan, has been serving as prime minister since 2002. But Turkey is unique in the region in having sustained a secular public culture for more than eight decades and democratic institutions for more than five. Moreover, contemporary Islamist moderation there may also stem from a tradition of state repression and intervention that has set clear limits on political behavior. Since Turkish Islamist parties began to participate in government in the 1970s, they have been banned and outlawed four times, and the Turkish military, the guardian of the secular republic, deposed an Islamic prime minister in 1997.

Among Arab countries, Jordan presents a model of successful Islamist co-optation (although less so of democracy). Islamists in Jordan were recognized publicly and given a stake in the political life there from the country's founding, in 1946, and as a result they have led the most establishment-oriented and least violent Islamist movement in the region. The Muslim Brotherhood in Jordan has channeled its energies into nonviolent activism and anti-U.S. and anti-Israel rhetoric, generally invoking sharia in moral rather than political affairs. Jordan's Islamists have stood by the monarchy's Hashemite ruling family in moments of crisis, such as the showdown with Palestinian armed groups in 1970-71 and the al Qaeda bombings in Amman last November. And since entering the formal political system by running in the parliamentary elections of 1989, the Muslim Brotherhood in Jordan has occupied, through its political wing, the Islamic Action Front, an average of a third of the seats in parliament.

It has been more common for regimes in the region to deal with Islamists through repression and confrontation followed by partial and limited co-optation. The Muslim Brotherhood in Egypt, for example (established in 1928), which favored violence to the point of assassinating a prime minister in 1948, was outlawed in 1954. Decades of repression and political exclusion eventually split the movement into two branches. The radicals found their way into Egyptian Islamic Jihad and ultimately al Qaeda. The moderates moved toward the mainstream, focused their message on education and the "indoctrination of the heart," and renounced the use of violence in 1971. They were then allowed to enter the political field, and they began participating in elections in 1984 (although they have had to run as independents, since Egyptian law bans parties based on religion). Relying on strong organizational skills and the good reputation of its social and religious arms, and taking advantage of the government's poor performance, the Muslim Brotherhood is now Egypt's leading opposition group.

Lebanon offers yet another model, with a strong Islamist movement (Hezbollah) operating with sponsorship from an external power (Iran) within a weak and fragmented political system. Hezbollah now maintains the most powerful militia in the country, with control of a virtually autonomous area in southern Lebanon and a global terrorist reach that has often served Iranian purposes. It has also become a central player in Lebanese politics, drawing on its base in the Shiite community, the largest community in the country. Syria's departure from Lebanon last April created a new freedom in Lebanese politics, and after enhancing its parliamentary representation in the May 2005 elections, Hezbollah joined the government for the first time. It has indeed found itself under pressure to disarm but, thanks to its newfound political power, has been able to fend off such pressure so far. Joining the government did not prevent Hezbollah from undertaking a serious cross-border attack on Israel in late November 2005, nor has its ideological platform or political demeanor shown signs of moderation. Whether, when, or under what conditions it will ultimately disarm remains to be seen.

Conditions and Context

The most important lesson to be drawn from these cases is that co-optation through political participation is not a given, but rather depends on the existence of certain conditions in the local political context. No Islamist movement has renounced violence or moderated its ideology of its own volition; when one has done so at all, it has been for lack of a better alternative. It appears that at least three factors need to be present for co-optation to occur: the existence of a strong, healthy, and relatively free political system into which the Islamists can be absorbed; a balance of power tilted against the Islamists that forces them to play by moderate rules; and sufficient time for co-optation to take effect.

A strong and healthy political system is essential because only it will offer Islamists the incentives for proper socialization. Unless elections are free and fair enough for the results to accurately reflect the popular will, there is little reason for a party to compete for new constituencies or marginal voters rather than cater to its extremist base. And unless the political order is stable and the state enforces a monopoly on authority and violence, there is little reason for a party to disarm (and much reason for it not to).

An imbalance of power favoring the state and mainstream forces is vital, meanwhile, because without checks and balances, a party inclined toward radicalism will be able to capture the state apparatus and bend it to its will. The Turkish army and the Jordanian monarchy have thus contributed to the eventual moderation of their countries' Islamists by setting limits on the kind of behavior permitted.

Many established democracies have also set up legislative roadblocks to help contain the political havoc that radical parties can wreak. In the wake of World War II, for example, a number of European countries barred outright certain types of parties to prevent a resurgence of fascism. In 1948, the first Israeli prime minister, David Ben-Gurion, forcibly crushed partisan armed movements in order to prevent them from poisoning the new Israeli democracy, and the Israeli legislature later excluded violent extremists.

And in 1984, then President Chaim Herzog (my late father), refused to meet with Meir Kahane, the leader of the ultranationalist Kach Party, even though Kahane had been elected to parliament—a stance that helped expand the legislative requirements of acceptability in Israel to include the rejection of racism and the endorsement of democracy.

Time is critical, finally, because ingrained habits of political moderation tend to be learned not in a day, but only through sustained experience over several years and several electoral cycles. It took several decades, for example, for the Egyptian Muslim Brotherhood to renounce violence. And in Ireland, it took a full seven years after the 1998 Good Friday agreement for the IRA to actually decommission its arms.

Unfortunately, if one looks closely at the case of Hamas, hardly any of these potentially moderating factors are present. Elections in the PA may be relatively free. But Palestinian political, security, and other institutions are a chaotic mess, and the pragmatic political center, represented by Fatah, is in complete disarray. Hamas is launching its political career in the legislative and executive branches without having disarmed and is quite possibly stronger than the rest of the state apparatus. Despite Abbas' occasional promises that he will force Hamas to disarm, no domestic player will be able to check the group's extremist tendencies, nor will any rules or safeguards be in place to proscribe unacceptable behavior.

In fact, all past Palestinian thresholds for political participation have been lifted. The 1995 Israeli-Palestinian Interim Agreement on the West Bank and the Gaza Strip introduced just such a threshold, with Hamas in mind. In Annex II, Article III(2), it disqualified from Palestinian elections "any candidates, parties or coalitions . . . [that] commit or advocate racism or pursue the implementation of their aims by unlawful or nondemocratic means." Yet the Palestinian election law for the 2006 elections, enacted in June 2005, contains no substantive rules by which candidates or parties have to abide.

The ongoing Palestinian-Israeli conflict, meanwhile, adds fuel to the fire of domestic Palestinian turmoil and to extremism. It provides an excuse for tolerating private armies within the PA and enhances the legitimacy of Hamas' rejectionist stance. Opinion polls show that although most Palestinians disagree with Hamas' ideological extremism and support a two-state solution to the conflict, they also accept the notion of "armed struggle" as a legitimate route to get there, citing the Israeli withdrawal from Gaza as an example of what such pressure can achieve. This complicated preference structure gives Hamas a perverse incentive to disrupt progress in diplomatic negotiations, since the normalization of Palestinian-Israeli relations could well lessen Hamas' appeal. As long as its military and political power enhance each other, Hamas will be able to fend off pressures to disarm and will derail progress toward peace. Given the urgency of moving the conflict toward resolution, finally, there simply is no time to let Palestinian domestic politics play out long enough for Hamas' political socialization to occur.

Heir Conditioning

It is too late to prevent an unreconstructed Hamas from participating in Palestinian politics. It is not too late, however, to avoid compounding that mistake by giving the group a continued free ride and full legitimacy regardless of its behavior from now on. The Palestinians, with the help of Israel, the United States, and the rest of the international community, should now try hard to create the conditions under which Hamas may liberalize, in the hope that one day the optimists might be proved right. This, obviously, is a long-term project.

With Hamas controlling Palestinian politics and national institutions, the immediate onus has shifted to outside players to create real incentives for Hamas to abandon its militancy and real disincentives to preserve it. The international community was poised to invest a tremendous amount of political and financial capital in promoting domestic Palestinian reform. Those investments should now be provided only if they can be used to equip moderates to compete more effectively with Hamas in both the security and social spheres. Aid should also be designed to create a pragmatic Palestinian political center by revamping Fatah and encouraging reform-minded activists and parties.

Outside actors should also try to use their influence to create the proper incentives and disincentives for Hamas' future behavior. The fact that so many Palestinians regard the group as entirely legitimate does not mean that all other interested parties have to agree. The international community should therefore clearly assert that in its eyes, democratic participation will confer legitimacy on Hamas only so long as the group renounces violence, disarms, and recognizes Israel's right to exist. Political engagement with Hamas and the removal of it from international terrorist lists should be made contingent on real progress in these areas, not simply on the group's willingness to enter the political field.

Ideally, Israeli-Palestinian relations would need to improve in tandem with conditions in the PA, so as to create a virtuous cycle that can help drive both the peace process and the Palestinian reform process forward. Because of the nature of Hamas and the threat of terrorism, final-status negotiations now seem as remote as ever. The transition of political leadership in Israel together with Hamas' newfound prominence will make extensive bilateral talks of any kind unlikely in the near term. The specter of a weak, dysfunctional PA coupled with a strong, violent Hamas is likely to deepen Israelis' inclination toward unilateralism in their relations with the Palestinians.

Ultimately, no outside party can substitute for the Palestinian leadership in creating what the New York Times columnist Thomas Friedman has called "the village": a domestic environment that can truly delegitimize extremism. The momentous experiment of allowing Hamas to enter democratic politics is only beginning, but even at this early point, the short-term dynamics seem bleak enough to undermine the project's long-term prospects. The time for taming Hamas may already have passed.

The Hamas Conundrum

Michael Herzog

In the four years since it swept Palestinian parliamentary elections, Hamas has neither moderated its policies nor adopted democratic principles. Constantly torn between its ideology as an Islamist jihadi movement and its responsibilities as a governing authority in the Gaza Strip, Hamas has proven unwilling to transform itself. The result has been an ongoing ideological and political crisis for Hamas and, more generally, the Palestinian Authority. Last October, Hamas was faced with the challenge of new elections mandated by Palestinian law and set for January by the Palestinian Authority president, Mahmoud Abbas, whose Fatah faction is Hamas' chief rival. Hamas' reaction was to ban any voting from taking place in Gaza. Consequently, Abbas postponed the elections indefinitely, sparking heated debate with Hamas over the legitimacy of his continued tenure as president.

Soon after Hamas' 2006 electoral victory, I identified some conditions necessary for co-opting ideologically extreme and violent political movements ("Can Hamas Be Tamed?" March/April 2006). I argued that Hamas was unlikely to become more moderate in the foreseeable future, primarily because there was neither a strong Palestinian government nor a viable political center capable of

---

MICHAEL HERZOG, a Brigadier General in the Israel Defense Forces, is a special emissary to the Israeli Prime Minister and Minister of Defense for the Middle East peace process. He served as Chief of Staff to the Israeli Minister of Defense from 2006 to 2009 and was a Fellow at the Washington Institute for Near East Policy from 2004 to 2006.

containing and co-opting the group. Unfortunately, this has proven to be true—and it remains so today.

After winning the 2006 election, Hamas immediately began grappling with various conflicting pressures. The Israeli government, which evacuated its citizens and military from Gaza in 2005, reacted strongly—militarily, economically, and diplomatically—to the continued firing of rockets from Gaza into southern Israel, first by factions other than Hamas and later by Hamas itself. Meanwhile, immediately after Hamas' electoral victory, the Quartet (the United States, the European Union, the United Nations, and Russia) demanded that Hamas, in order to gain international legitimacy, commit to nonviolence, recognize Israel, and accept previous agreements signed between Israel and the Palestinian Authority. All the while, Hamas felt a domestic imperative to secure Palestinian national unity. In the face of these pressures, it consistently tried to govern without moderating its ideology. It remained dedicated to "resistance" and to Israel's destruction—and therefore opposed to any concept of a real peace process.

When forced to make hard choices, Hamas has been repeatedly pulled down by the weight of its dogma. In early 2007, in an attempt to halt escalating intra-Palestinian bloodshed and secure international aid, Hamas agreed to share power with Fatah in a national unity government. But Hamas adamantly refused to include in the government's platform any acceptance of the Quartet's conditions or of the 2002 Arab peace initiative, which proposed that Arab states normalize relations with Israel following a comprehensive settlement of Arab-Israeli issues. By June 2007, the national unity government had collapsed. Under the initiative of its more radical military wing, Hamas forcibly overran Gaza and brutally established its rule, in many cases throwing Fatah members from rooftops or shooting them in the knees. Thus, despite the expectations of some who encouraged Hamas' participation in politics, political inclusion did not contain or domesticate the group. Rather, Hamas resisted domestication until finally bursting out and forming an independent political entity.

The violent end of the unity government split the Palestinian territories into two entities—one in the West Bank, one in the Gaza Strip—with vastly different governments and political climates. In the West Bank, Abbas and Salam Fayyad, the Palestinian Authority prime minister, embarked on an overdue and unprecedented reform process, which included clamping down on Hamas grassroots groups through widespread arrests, the discharging of radical preachers from mosques, and the seizure of Hamas funds. The reform effort has brought improved security and impressive economic growth to the West Bank. In Gaza, by contrast, Hamas focused on being the flag-bearer for Islamists in the Middle East. This attitude led the group to cast aside practical realities in favor of pursuing ideological goals. In addition to forcing itself on local clans and usurping traditional power bases, Hamas initiated a gradual yet determined process of Islamization in all spheres of life. These included legislation and the courts; the education system; the media; and social life, as the group, in accordance with its Islamic code of conduct, demanded "modest" dress for women, banned mixed-gender social events, closed or monitored Internet cafés, and even condemned chewing gum because it "arouses the passion of the youth." Hamas' Islamization has also meant the systematic persecution of Gaza's Christians. As Abbas recently put it, Hamas' policies turned Gaza into "an emirate of darkness."

Despite this record, debate still persisted among Western commentators over whether Hamas was becoming moderate. This was because Hamas performed some window dressing to maintain its domestic legitimacy and garner international approval. Over the last two years, it has been conducting intermittent national unity talks with Fatah (to no avail). It also reached out to the West, suggesting a dialogue with Western governments. And some Hamas leaders occasionally expressed willingness to accept a long-term cease-fire with Israel if a Palestinian state were established along the 1967 borders. Hamas assumed these seemingly moderate postures as a way to address political pressures without reforming its ideology: there has been no evidence that Hamas leaders are reconsidering their core beliefs—only that they are, at most, debating which tactics best serve those beliefs.

After Israel's pullout from Gaza, one of Hamas' main tactics was to allow, and later orchestrate, the regular firing of rockets from Gaza into nearby Israeli towns. Eventually, in December 2008, this rocket fire provoked Israel to launch Operation Cast Lead, a massive military operation in Gaza. It dealt a crippling blow to Hamas and deterred further rocket fire: whereas 7,000 rockets and mortar shells were fired into Israel in the three years before the operation, only about 300 were fired in the 12 months following January 2009, as Hamas has enforced a near-total cease-fire since Operation Cast Lead ended that month.

At the same time, however, Hamas has been rearming, especially with long-range rockets, despite enhanced Egyptian efforts to curb the smuggling of weapons through tunnels under the Egypt-Gaza border. Hamas is helped in this smuggling effort by Iran. In October 2009, Hamas test-fired an Iranian-manufactured rocket capable of hitting Israel's largest city, Tel Aviv.

This history and the fact that the group seems to be ignoring strong pressures to reform—including rising domestic unpopularity and an unprecedented crisis in relations with Egypt—suggest that Hamas cannot be part of an Israeli-Palestinian peace process based on recognizing Israel and making historic compromises, nor part of a Palestinian body politic based on democracy and free elections.

Reaching a temporary cease-fire with Israel and claiming willingness to accept a Palestinian state within the 1967 borders is no true sign of moderation when Hamas is simultaneously building its arsenal and treating terrorism as a tactical tool. "Hamas will never give up the option of resistance," the Hamas political chief Khaled Mashal stated at a rally last month, "no matter how long it takes." Hamas' seemingly moderate political statements are always accompanied by forbidding conditions—for example, that in exchange for only a cease-fire on Hamas' part (not the recognition of Israel),

Israel would have to withdraw to the 1967 lines and accept all Palestinian refugees.

Likewise, participating in the 2006 elections and flirting with national unity arrangements is not proof that Hamas has accepted the rules of democracy. The real test of a ruling party is if it agrees to a second round of elections, even if it might lose. Hamas failed that test recently when it undermined the scheduled Palestinian presidential and parliamentary elections.

The sad conclusion is that Hamas presents one of those policy problems that are only manageable, not solvable. No force in Palestinian politics today has the power to break Hamas' ideological basis or grip on power in Gaza. For internal pressure to be effective—that is, for it to move Hamas to become more moderate, relinquish violence, endorse the peace process, and embrace democratic practices—it would have to be coupled with solid, sustained external pressure. If international powers, led by the United States and the other members of the Quartet, grant Hamas a free pass, the group will continue to play the spoiler, threaten Abbas and other moderates in the West Bank, and serve Iranian interests.

No matter what, changing Hamas will be a long-term journey, like any process of co- optation. The challenge is to manage it in a way that mitigates the impact on innocent Palestinians, minimizes the risk of all-out escalation, and leaves room for a viable peace process. These imperatives, in turn, underscore the urgency of re-launching the peace process under a supportive Arab umbrella that, based on shared concerns over Iran's bellicosity, would foster moderation and stability in the face of extremism. But the policy conundrum remains: Will the peace process progress with Hamas, or in spite of it? Unless Hamas unexpectedly changes course, the group will exclude itself from the process. That would be for the better. The challenge for policymakers in Washington, Europe, Jerusalem, and Ramallah then becomes how to deny Hamas the capacity to play the spoiler.

Letter From Gaza: Hamas the Opportunist

Hamas' Tunnel Diplomacy

Thanassis Cambanis

The thousands of traders who swarm the once destitute corridor that marks Gaza's southernmost boundary with Egypt call the area the "Rafah free zone." They spend most of their day in hot, damp passageways a hundred feet underground, dragging rubber sleighs loaded with goods and then winching them to the surface.

Rafah long languished as a provincial backwater in the claustrophobic Gaza Strip, a clannish and rural hinterland to Gaza City's bustling and cosmopolitan downtown. A few families controlled the limited tunnel trade that existed for decades. And even in the days when Gaza's legal overland trade flourished, weapons and contraband were still smuggled into the Strip underground.

At first, in 2007, Hamas only tolerated the tunnel economy; but it began to embrace it the following year, legalizing and regulating subterranean trade. Hamas had found a spontaneous solution to the economic crisis that was threatening its rule of Gaza—and, in the process, turned expediency into opportunity.

Opportunism as strategy appears to be the group's new hallmark. When faced with only bad options to deal with the blockade

THANNASIS CAMBANIS is the author of *A Privilege to Die: Inside Hezbollah's Legions and Their Endless War Against Israel*, which will be published in September.

or its status as a diplomatic pariah, Hamas has behaved as if it chose its predicament, leveraging its position into either greater control over Gaza or greater political influence beyond its boundaries. Desperation, in other words, has become an avenue to power.

The snaking tunnels, like Hamas' contorted diplomatic campaign, grew out of the total isolation the movement faced after it won the 2006 Palestinian parliamentary elections. Israel and the United States both list Hamas as a terrorist group and immediately boycotted the new Hamas government. In the summer of 2007, Hamas took over Gaza after a quick but bloody clash with U.S.-trained forces from the Fatah faction. Since then, Israel has closed off all but the most basic trade and movement.

In response, Hamas moved to legalize the tunnels, charging licensing fees and opening up the "free zone" to a group of investors who would owe their profits and livelihoods to Hamas. Hundreds of new tunnels have opened every year since 2008. "We have run out of land for new tunnels," Major Rafaat Salama, the police chief, cheerily told me.

Abu Tarek, now 32 years old, has worked in the tunnels his entire adult life. In three years, he has gone from poor laborer to middle-class contractor, one of the countless unintended beneficiaries of Israel's blockade. "Before, it used to be a terrifying business," he told me, standing at the mouth of one of the tunnels he had dug.

Now, Hamas police officers patrol the 1,000-plus tunnels, and Hamas officials adjudicate labor disputes. When tunnel workers die in the not infrequent "workplace accidents," Hamas specifies how much the employers must pay the survivors—usually between $12,000 and $20,000, depending on the worker's age and number of children.

The main goal of the blockade, Israel says, is to prevent Hamas from importing weapons and dual-use material—cement, for example, could be used to build bunkers, and pipes to manufacture rockets. The blockade's secondary aim is to weaken Hamas by making life under its rule unpleasant for Gazans—hence the bans on jam, cilantro, toys, and paper. Regardless, Gaza's merchants can get virtually anything, even cars, through the tunnels. Diesel and gas flow through jerry-rigged pipelines. Vendors at Gaza's markets sell essential goods such as tiles and cement, food staples such as sea bass and fresh oranges, and relative luxuries such as French yogurt and the Swiss toothbrushes that I bought for a dollar each.

Nonetheless, Gaza is a depressing place. Almost nobody leaves, and most people do not work. The siege of Gaza might not look like the siege of Stalingrad, but a siege it is. The tunnels still do not solve the fundamental problems of the blockade, including the absence of the supplies and machinery necessary to repair Gaza's worn and war-shattered infrastructure (such as its sewage treatment system, power plants, and schools, to name a few of the top priorities cited by the United Nations). But they have solved Hamas' short-term problem: staving off the popular rage that seethed during the blockade's peak.

The tunnels are also the best illustration of how Hamas has learned to govern. Along the way to creating a new class of siege millionaires, it experimented with and discarded many approaches: firing rockets, adhering to a cease-fire, bringing millions in cash from Arab capitals in briefcases, railing against Israel, and partnering with smugglers. Finally, it legalized the tunnel economy. Since Israel has claimed that it will end the Gaza blockade only if Hamas surrenders power, the movement has been willing to improvise and embrace whatever works—a merchant's approach of finding the best deal and then justifying it retroactively.

Hamas has applied the same formula to its diplomatic strategy. It has hedged its bets, alternately hectoring and wooing Egypt, cozying up to Iran and Turkey, and shaming the Gulf petro-states into giving it money and political cover. In January, Gaza's prime minister, Ismail Haniyeh, chastised Egypt from the minbar at Friday prayers in Gaza City for "losing its compass" and joining the ranks of those who "criminalize the resistance." The Arabs, he argued, must draw close to Turkey: "We are working to build a new balance against the Israelis in the region."

Since the 2006 elections, Hamas' brain trust has been trying to plot a path out of global isolation. Ahmed Yousef leads the effort, drawing on his experience running an Islamic think tank in what he calls the "paradise" of Washington, D.C., for more than a decade. The number-two official in Hamas' foreign ministry in Gaza, he is at once a consummate politician and a fierce defender of Hamas' resistance ideology. He may be a conciliator, but he is no moderate.

"We want the West to understand it can do business with us," he told me in January during a long conversation in his Gaza City office. "They want to know if we are more like the Taliban or like [Turkey's Islamist prime minister, Recep Tayyip] Erdogan. They will see that we are closer to Erdogan. We are flexible."

Diplomatically, Hamas has cast a wide net. The group has launched Web sites in English and Turkish and has dispatched senior officials to meet with any influential Westerners willing to talk, in public or in secret. Now, Hamas is benefiting from the results of its diplomatic groundwork. The flotilla that it did not organize has played right to Hamas' strategy, earning it a spate of attention and summoning international pressure on Israel to loosen the blockade.

In the waning years of the Bush administration, Yousef contends, the White House sent "track two" emissaries to find out if Hamas was willing to change its ways. It was not, but Hamas officials were deeply interested in continuing a dialogue with Washington. More recently, Hamas passed a letter to the White House by hiding it in U.S. Senator John Kerry's UN briefing packet. And last June, a group of former senior U.S. diplomats joined European officials at a two-day meeting with Hamas leaders in Zurich. Such contacts have continued, sources familiar with the talks have told me.

"These are the players on our playground. We are there, ready to deal," Yousef said. "We would like to be engaged. We are willing to sit and talk. We want to be part of a peaceful attempt to settle the conflict." Whether or not he is sincere, both Israel and the

United States distrust Hamas' overtures, in large part because the movement refuses to repudiate violence, including attacks on civilians.

Using a combination of guile, violence, and diplomacy, Hamas believes it can implement its own roadmap to an enduring cease-fire (which is its goal, it should be said, as opposed to "peace"). First in this plan, Hamas wants to expand the circle of countries that support it and chip away at the bloc opposing it. Turkey so far has proved the most responsive.

Second, it wants to reconcile with Egypt, which seems to loathe Hamas as much as Israel does, mostly because of the internal threat the country faces from Hamas' parent group, the Muslim Brotherhood. Third, it wants to rejoin the Palestinian Authority on equal or superior terms to Fatah, which it defeated in the 2006 elections. Fourth, Hamas wants to begin talks with Israel based on the equilibrium that prevailed before the most recent Gaza war: a temporary truce that would allow the two sides to discuss a lasting cessation of hostilities and a return to the 1967 borders. Hamas' long-term strategy does not aim for a final resolution but rather an indefinite cease-fire, with two neighbors living in a grudging coexistence (much as, say, Israel and Lebanon do today).

Hamas has defied the expectations of policymakers in Israel and the United States, first by digging its way out of economic ruin with the surprisingly resilient tunnel economy, then by diverting attention from its dark and violent side during the current unraveling of the consensus for a complete Hamas boycott. In both cases, Hamas went around and through the problem rather than confronting it head-on. For the time being, Hamas has survived without dealing with its own vulnerabilities, including its anti-Semitic charter, its disregard for the laws of war, and its propensity for authoritarianism. As Israel and the United States are beginning to learn, Hamas is a strategic actor that, for all its rough edges, knows how to engage in diplomacy. Its goals might be as belligerent as ever, but its tactics are increasingly pragmatic and effective. Washington and Israel might choose not to deal with Hamas, but Hamas is dealing with them.

How to Handle Hamas

The Perils of Ignoring Gaza's Leadership

Daniel Byman

The biggest obstacle to peace between the Israelis and the Palestinians is not the Palestinians' demand that Jewish settlements in the West Bank be dismantled, the barrier separating much of the West Bank from Israel, or the recent rightward shift of the Israeli body politic. It is the emergence of Hamas as the de facto government of the Gaza Strip, where 1.5 million Palestinians reside.

Hamas has regularly attacked Israel with rockets from Gaza or allowed others to do so. It poses a strong and growing political threat to the more moderate Palestinian Authority, which is led by President Mahmoud Abbas and his technocratic prime minister, Salam Fayyad, and which governs the West Bank and used to run Gaza, too. Whereas PA leaders see negotiations with Israel and institution building as the best way to ultimately gain statehood, Hamas seeks to undermine the peace process.

Many Hamas members have not reconciled themselves to the Jewish state's existence. Hamas' leaders also fear that Hamas would reap none of the benefits of a peace deal and that in the event of one, the PA would score political points at their expense. Hamas

DANIEL BYMAN is a Professor in the Security Studies Program at Georgetown University and a Senior Fellow at the Saban Center for Middle East Policy at the Brookings Institution. He is the author of the forthcoming book *A High Price: The Triumphs and Failures of Israeli Counterterrorism*.

has shown repeatedly that it can bring talks to a painful end by castigating moderate Palestinians and turning to violence.

Despite Hamas' centrality to Israeli security and Palestinian politics, Washington still clings to the policy that the Bush administration established after Hamas beat more moderate Fatah candidates in elections in Gaza in 2006. The United States and other members of the international community withdrew development aid from Gaza, tacitly supporting Israel's shutdown of the Gaza Strip, and refused to work directly with Hamas. Their hope was to force Hamas' collapse and bring Fatah back to power. But isolation has failed, and today Hamas is far stronger than when it first took power. The Obama administration, more by default than by design, has continued these efforts to isolate and weaken Hamas, opposing talks with the group and condoning Israeli military raids.

Israeli policy also remains stuck in the past. Regular rocket barrages from Gaza mean that Israel cannot simply forget about the area or Hamas. Israel has kept Gaza under siege and has sometimes used considerable force. Although the Gaza war of December 2008 and January 2009 (which Israelis call Operation Cast Lead) did damage Hamas' credibility, and even though Hamas has since reduced its rocket attacks, the long-term sustainability of such an aggressive approach is questionable. Still, Israel and the international community have not developed a new strategy in response to Hamas' consolidation of power.

Some prominent Israelis, such as Efraim Halevy, the former director of Mossad, the Israeli secret service, and Giora Eiland, a former head of Israel's National Security Council, have called for negotiating with Hamas. Other Israelis, who fear that the group will never abandon its goal of destroying Israel, think the Israeli military should retake Gaza before Hamas gets any stronger; they argue that postponing the day of reckoning will cost Israel dearly in the future. But with neither option being palatable at this time, Israel continues to rely on economic pressure and military operations to preempt terrorist attacks from Gaza, kill the people there who launch rockets into Israel, and retaliate for Hamas' provocations.

Although shunning Hamas may seem morally appropriate and politically safe, that policy will undermine Israel's peace talks with Abbas and other Palestinian moderates. An alternative approach is necessary. Hamas could, perhaps, be convinced not to undermine progress on a peace deal. To accomplish this, Israel and the international community would have to exploit Hamas' vulnerabilities, particularly its performance in governing Gaza, with a mix of coercion and concessions, including a further easing of the siege of Gaza. At the same time, they should support the state-building efforts of Fayyad and restart the peace process with Abbas in order to reduce the risk that Hamas will win the struggle for power among the Palestinians. Moreover, because the effort to transform Hamas into a responsible government could fail, the international community must be prepared to support a more aggressive military response by Israel if Hamas does not change.

The Eve of Disruption

Peace talks can begin with Hamas on the sidelines, but they cannot finish if Hamas refuses to play ball. Hamas has proved that it has the means to threaten Israel and disrupt peace talks. Rocket and mortar strikes are the most obvious method. According to Israeli government statistics, in 2005, Hamas and other Palestinian groups launched around 850 rockets and mortars at Israel from Gaza. By 2008, the figure had climbed past 2,000. The death toll from these attacks was low, but the psychological effect has been considerable. Hamas uses Qassam rockets, which have unpredictable trajectories and so fall on soldiers and civilians alike. One 2007 study found that 28 percent of the adults and between 72 percent and 94 percent of the children in Sderot, the Israeli town most frequently hit by rockets, suffered from posttraumatic stress disorder.

In addition to the rocket attacks, Hamas and other militant groups shoot at Israeli soldiers and agricultural workers near the Gaza border. From 2000, when the second intifada broke out, through 2009, there were over 5,000 such attacks from Gaza. The vast majority occurred before Israel withdrew from Gaza in 2005, but Israel still suffered more than 70 attacks in each of the three years that followed. A particularly difficult problem has been Hamas' use of improvised explosive devices near the security barrier. These bombs are powerful enough to endanger Israeli soldiers patrolling the Israeli side but can only be dismantled from the Gaza side.

Attacks by Hamas plummeted following Operation Cast Lead, a tough, sometimes brutal three-week campaign against Gaza carried out by Israel in December 2008 and January 2009; it ended with a cease-fire on both sides. After March 2009, no month of that year saw more than 25 rocket and mortar attacks—a far cry from the violence of 2008. There were only four shootings in 2009. So far, 2010 has seen a comparatively low number of rockets flying from Gaza—few, if any, of which were launched by Hamas itself.

But few attacks is not the same as no attacks. The Israelis still fear that Hamas, which is building its capabilities, could easily step up the violence if it chose to do so. For the Israelis, engaging in peace talks premised on giving up territory is difficult when their country is under attack; they justifiably feel the need to hit back. The Israelis also worry that Hamas or another Palestinian group would launch rockets from any territory that Israel surrendered in the West Bank, just as they did from Gaza after Israel withdrew its forces in 2005.

For moderate Palestinian officials seeking peace, the challenge goes beyond Israeli fears. Israel and the international community, of course, recognize that Abbas does not control Hamas. But if violence again flared up, the Israelis would question the value of peace talks with moderates if they cannot end the violence. Israel does not respond to every attack, but when it does it often hits back hard, killing Hamas leaders and, inadvertently but regularly, civilians, too. Moderate Palestinian officials would find it impossible to gain popular support for negotiations while Palestinian civilians were dying at the hands of Israelis. So even when its attacks do no damage Hamas walks away triumphant, whereas both Israeli and Palestinian moderates are discredited.

Hamas is also capable of kidnapping personnel from the Israel Defense Forces or other Israelis: a rare but game-changing event. The most dramatic incident was the June 2006 abduction of the Israeli soldier Gilad Shalit. Israeli society rallied behind Shalit's family, and the IDF invaded Gaza in an operation that killed over 400 Palestinians and failed to secure Shalit's release. The kidnapping also helped convince then Prime Minister Ehud Olmert to attack Hezbollah in Lebanon after Hezbollah kidnapped two Israeli soldiers in July 2006. In circumstances like these, negotiations are almost impossible.

Further complicating the picture is Hamas' ability to undermine peace talks without using violence itself. Gaza is home to various other terrorist groups, from Fatah rejectionists to Salafi jihadist organizations, none remotely as strong as Hamas but all itching to attack Israel. Hamas can allow these groups to operate and then claim impotence or ignorance. It can also stymie negotiations politically. Hamas lambasted Abbas for meeting with Israeli officials and for not demanding that the UN endorse the findings of the Goldstone report, which criticized Israel's conduct of Operation Cast Lead. Hamas uses such attacks to "prove" to Palestinians that Abbas is selling out the Palestinian cause. Such charges make it harder for Abbas to consider making any concessions to Israel, particularly the type that involve no immediate quid pro quos from Israel or, worse, that mean swallowing rebuffs or tolerating continued settlement building.

For now, Hamas does not have to do much to scuttle peace talks: disagreements over settlements and other disputes have left the Israelis and the PA unable to get anything going beyond indirect talks brokered by Washington. Both sides view these talks with considerable skepticism. But should negotiations move forward, as the Obama administration is urging, Hamas is likely to play the spoiler. Progress on negotiations with Israel would make the Palestinian moderates look good and pose a threat to Hamas' standing among Palestinians by reducing the appeal of its ideological hostility toward Israel.

Skeptics might contend that peace talks have often occurred without Hamas' participation. Since the second intifada, Washington has tried to move the ball forward from time to time, but any resulting talks made so little progress that Hamas did not perceive them as a serious threat. When talks were near fruition in the mid-1990s, however, Hamas—much weaker then—struck. In 1996, Hamas and Palestinian Islamic Jihad (PIJ) launched a series of suicide bombings against Israel. These not only killed over 60 Israelis but also shattered the prospects of Prime Minister Shimon Peres and his pro-peace bloc in upcoming elections, paving the way for the triumph of Benjamin Netanyahu, who was far more skeptical of negotiations. Terror has worked for Hamas, and it might be tempted to use the tactic again.

The Isolation of Gaza
Israel, Egypt, and the international community have put Gaza under siege to isolate and weaken Hamas. Israel has sealed off Gaza from the sea, and the crossing points into it from Israel and Egypt have usually been closed to normal traffic. Humanitarian aid goes in, but there is a long list of prohibited goods. Ironically, however, Israel's humanitarian concerns have prevented it from truly pressuring the Gazan people. Israel has tried to coerce Hamas without causing mass starvation, an approach that Israeli officials have described as "no prosperity, no development, no humanitarian crisis." Although Israeli policies are pushing Gaza closer to the brink, the threat of even more misery simply is not credible.

This is small comfort to Gazans, however. Aid agencies now put Gaza's poverty rate at 80 percent, and most Gazans survive on UN handouts and aid from Hamas' patrons, such as Iran. The World Health Organization reported at the beginning of this year that hospitals are unable to deliver quality health care; their doctors, unable to receive training. Disease and malnutrition are spreading, and schools are deteriorating. Gazans, who for decades took menial jobs in Israel, lost access to the Israeli labor market after violence flared during the second intifada. Subsequent border closures and the collapse of aid and investment have further decreased employment.

The world lays the blame for this humanitarian catastrophe at Israel's feet. After UN Secretary-General Ban Ki-moon visited Gaza in March 2010, for example, he declared Israeli policy "wrong," contending that it was causing "unacceptable suffering." Still, except during Operation Cast Lead, the siege received only limited attention until recently.

The spotlight focused again on Gaza on May 31, 2010, when Israeli commandos stormed the *Mavi Marmara*, a civilian Turkish ship trying to break the blockade, and killed nine activists. Turkish leaders, already at odds with their once close ally over Operation Cast Lead, denounced the raid, demanded an apology, and took reprisals, including the decision to close Turkish airspace to Israeli aircraft. British Prime Minister David Cameron said the raid was "completely unacceptable," and Obama administration officials called for "a new approach to Gaza." Soon, the botched raid became a broader fiasco for Israel. It put global attention back on the siege of Gaza. Israel's restrictions of innocuous items, such as cilantro and jam, came under increased scrutiny. Worse, Hamas started to look like it was the victim of Israeli cruelty and violence.

To appease critics after the *Mavi Marmara* bungling, Israel declared that it would focus on military-related goods only and promised to make it easier for Gazans to seek medical care outside the Gaza Strip. But it maintained a ban on "dual-use" items, which could include goods ranging from electronics to construction materials, depending on how the term is interpreted. Egypt, for its part, opened the Rafah crossing to allow humanitarian aid into Gaza and to admit into Egypt Gazans seeking medical care. But Cairo remains eager to avoid helping Hamas unless forced to by public opinion and, significantly, is continuing work on a wall along and under its border with Gaza. Easing Egypt's and Israel's siege would lessen Gazans' misery somewhat and help Hamas politically, but the Gaza Strip still has a long way to go before it is not a basket case.

Help for Hamas

The siege has failed on another level: it has not weakened Hamas, which has by now crushed or outflanked its political rivals. Today, Hamas has an unquestioned—and, in the eyes of most Gazans, largely legitimate—monopoly on the use of force in the Gaza Strip, and its political clout among Palestinians has grown at the expense of Fatah. Hamas bases its claim to power on its victory in the 2006 elections, when it ran largely on a platform that stressed Fatah's corruption and failure to deliver either services on the ground or sovereignty at the negotiating table. Younger Palestinians, in particular, are disillusioned with Fatah: they prefer the new brand of political Islam to old-fashioned Arab nationalism. Meanwhile, the plunge in trade and investment in Gaza has hurt the small Gazan middle class and others who might otherwise have had the resources to stand up to Hamas.

The siege has also increased the importance of the social services that Hamas provides. After it took over the Gaza Strip in 2007, Hamas revamped the police and security forces, cutting them from 50,000 members (on paper, at least) under Fatah to smaller, more efficient forces of just over 10,000, which then cracked down on crime and gangs. No longer did groups openly carry weapons or steal with impunity. People paid their taxes and electric bills, and in return the authorities picked up garbage and put criminals in jail. Gaza—neglected under Egyptian and then Israeli control, and misgoverned by Palestinian leader Yasir Arafat and his successors—finally has a real government.

Despite the siege, Hamas is growing stronger militarily. Its rockets are getting more powerful and are reaching farther. Until 2008, the rocket attacks hit only the relatively unpopulated areas near Gaza, such as Sderot. Over time, however, Hamas tripled the range of the rockets; today, they can reach large nearby cities, such as Ashqelon and Beersheba—and possibly even Tel Aviv. And it is developing indigenous rocket systems that have an even longer range and a larger payload. Through illicit tunnels linking the Gaza Strip to Egypt, Hamas smuggles out hundreds of young men for advanced training in Lebanon and Iran. Its fighters are becoming more formidable.

Hamas has also found a way to benefit economically from the blockade by taxing the tunnel trade, even creating a "tunnels authority." Yezid Sayigh of King's College London has estimated that Hamas earned up to $200 million from tunnel taxes in 2009. The tunnels also employ over 40,000 people, creating an important business constituency for Hamas.

And thanks to Israel's blockade and military strikes against Gaza, Hamas has found it easier to raise money from Iran, which gives Hamas tens of millions of dollars a year as part of its struggle against Israel and to score points with ordinary Sunni Arabs who admire Hamas. Hamas is also beginning to look beyond pariahs such as Iran for backing. Khaled Mashaal, the group's so-called external leader, met with Russian President Dmitry Medvedev in Damascus in May. And together with Turkish President Abdullah Gül, they called for including Hamas in peace talks. The *Mavi Marmara* raid has accelerated Hamas' escape from diplomatic isolation, with more and more countries casting Hamas as the victim.

The siege is also dragging down U.S. policy toward the Muslim world. The suffering of Gazans—broadcast constantly on al Jazeera—acts as a radicalizing force from Morocco to Indonesia. Terrorists in the United States itself, such as Major Nidal Hasan, the Fort Hood shooter, and Faisal Shahzad, the Times Square bomber, cite Gaza to justify their actions. And as many Muslims see it, U.S. support for Israel's siege proves that the United States is anti-Palestinian. Although the Obama administration successfully pressed Israel to ease the blockade, the remaining restrictions and the general sense that the United States continues to be Israel's strongest ally have meant that this perception endures.

This perception would become stronger if a new military operation on the scale of Operation Cast Lead occurred—an ever-present risk. In part, this risk is random: the rockets that land in Sderot usually kill no one, but there is always a chance that one could kill children or harm enough adults that the Israeli government would feel political pressure to escalate the conflict. An even bigger problem for Israel is that the current cease-fire is now based on short-term deterrence rather than a long-term deal. Hamas has stopped attacking Israel not because it has agreed to a broader political arrangement but because the benefits outweigh the costs for now. The deterrence equation could easily be disrupted if, say, more arms went to Hamas or if politics in Israel or Gaza changed. In other words, the siege is failing even on its own terms: Hamas has become stronger politically and militarily.

The Limits of Force

Some Israelis believe that the alternative to the siege is to confront Hamas head-on, removing it from power and forcing it underground. But that strategy would lead Israel into a quagmire. Conquering Gaza would be a relatively easy task for the IDF, but it would almost certainly result in far more Israeli casualties than the 13 who died during Operation Cast Lead. The Palestinians lost over 1,000 Hamas fighters and civilians in Operation Cast Lead, and they, too, would probably lose far more. In Operation Cast Lead, Israel penetrated only partway into the Gaza Strip and did not stay and occupy the territory. If the IDF were to remove Hamas from power, however, it would have to stay for months to dismantle Hamas' infrastructure there: the hospitals, mosques, and social services that Hamas has been putting in place for decades. And it would not be cheap, since Israel would have to bear the financial burden of deploying thousands of troops to Gaza.

Diplomatically, occupying Gaza again would hurt Israel's relations with the United States, the international community, and Palestinians in the West Bank. Israel would inevitably make mistakes and kill innocent Gazans, making negotiations even more difficult. Hamas, meanwhile, would try to make the long-term price of any occupation too high for Israel to sustain. In Gaza itself, the organization could attack Israeli soldiers with snipers, improvised explosive devices, suicide bombs, and ambushes, and in the West

Bank it could use its operatives to strike Israel. All this would take a bloody toll on the Israeli military.

Another big political loser would be Abbas. When Israel invaded Gaza in December 2008, the credibility of both Abbas and Fayyad suffered; they called for a cease-fire rather than for the kind of violent opposition that Palestinian leaders had been extolling for years. At the time, many Palestinians believed, and correctly so, that Abbas was rooting for Israel and against his fellow Palestinians because he sought to gain a political advantage over Hamas. Public opinion polls taken before the war showed that the leader of Hamas, Ismail Haniyeh, would lose a presidential race against Abbas; polls taken after the war showed Haniyeh winning. Renewing the peace process with Abbas will be impossible if the IDF and Hamas are shooting at each other in Gaza. Abbas would not want to be seen as supporting the Israeli takeover, and he openly rejected such an option during Operation Cast Lead. But even if Abbas kept a low profile, Hamas would still see him as complicit and try to undermine his position in the West Bank.

Another problem is that Israel would lack staying power. Israel left Gaza in 2005 in the hopes of never returning, and it does not have the stomach for another grinding occupation. On the other hand, seizing Gaza again only to withdraw again would simply allow Hamas to retake power once more, because Hamas' moderate rivals in the Gaza Strip are too weak to take over. A new occupation is not the answer, and despite bluster to the contrary, most Israelis realize this.

Cease-Fire Calculus

If Hamas cannot be uprooted, can it be calmed enough to not disrupt peace talks? Maybe—and the chance is worth pursuing. Although often depicted as fanatical, Hamas has shown itself to be pragmatic in practice, although rarely in rhetoric. It cuts deals with rivals, negotiates indirectly with Israel via the Egyptians, and otherwise demonstrates that unlike, say, al Qaeda, it is capable of compromise. Indeed, al Qaeda often blasts Hamas for selling out.

Hamas has at times declared and adhered to cease- fires lasting months, and some leaders have speculated that a truce lasting years is possible. And although Hamas has refused to recognize Israel's right to exist, its leaders have also said they would accept the UN-demarcated 1967 borders between Israel and the Palestinian areas as a starting point for a Palestinian state. Perhaps the most important sign of pragmatism has been Hamas' general adherence to its cease-fire after Operation Cast Lead.

To be sure, there are many reasons why Hamas might undermine peace talks. Progress on negotiations would elevate Abbas' standing among Palestinians and threaten Hamas' position. More important, it would weaken Hamas' message that resistance is the path to victory. In the 1990s, support for Hamas rose and fell in inverse proportion to progress on the peace talks, and Abbas hopes that he can outdo Hamas by rebuilding Fatah's political position at the negotiating table. Thus, if serious peace talks begin soon without Israel's dealing with Hamas first, Hamas will have a political incentive to break the cease-fire—either directly or by granting groups such as the PIJ more leeway to attack Israel.

And even if Abbas and the peace process were taken out of the equation, formalizing a lasting cease-fire would be risky for Hamas. Doing so would damage Hamas' credentials as a resistance organization. That, in turn, would jeopardize Hamas' funding from Iran and weaken it relative to Abbas, since both would then be tarred with the brush of passivity. Pressure from al Qaeda-like jihadists, the PIJ, and Hamas' own military wing make it hard for Hamas' leaders to renounce violence, particularly openly.

Hamas would also risk alienating elements of the group outside Gaza. The organization has a major presence in the West Bank, where it did well in elections in 2005 and 2006, and much of its leadership and fundraising apparatus is based in Syria and other Arab and Western states. These facets of the organization, which are committed to violent resistance and focus on gaining power in all of historic Palestine, not just Gaza, would have to take a back seat while the emphasis is on Gaza.

All these concerns seemed insurmountable in the past. And although they remain serious, today there is hope that Hamas can be convinced to let the peace process move forward. Its biggest vulnerability stems from its biggest victory: its electoral win in 2006 and takeover of Gaza in 2007. Now that Hamas must govern and is responsible for the welfare of the Gazans, it can no longer simply be a resistance group, criticizing and undermining Abbas and other moderate Palestinian leaders, avoiding responsibility for tough decisions, and gleefully watching moderates get blamed when Israel retaliates for its acts of terrorism. Hamas learned this lesson during Operation Cast Lead, when Gazans criticized it for the devastation the IDF inflicted on Gaza. The Gazan public is firmly opposed to renewing the rocket attacks. The siege has not weakened Hamas' power, but it has forced the organization to become more realistic. Gazans are sick of empty slogans of resistance; giving them a better life will require Hamas to make compromises.

Although the siege of Gaza has weakened opposition to Hamas, it has also prevented Hamas from governing well and from proving to Palestinians in the West Bank and Arabs in general that Islamists can run a government. When Gaza came under Palestinian control in 1994, the poverty rate there was 16 percent, barely above that of the United States. In 2009, 70 percent of Gazans were living on less than $1 a day, according to the UN. Mundane concerns about making ends meet dominate the local agenda. As an International Crisis Group report quoted one Palestinian aid worker, "People in Gaza are more concerned with Karni [the crossing point to Israel] than al- Quds [Jerusalem], with access to medical care than the Dome of the Rock."

Iran, tunnel taxes, and Hamas' fundraising apparatus allow the movement to survive, but they are not enough to make Gaza prosper. Hamas cannot pay for all of Gaza's employees and projects. In the past, it spent money on sustaining its mosques, hospitals, personnel, and military. Now, however, it is responsible for all of Gaza—a much greater financial challenge. It is also difficult for Hamas to get currency into Gaza; it must smuggle it in from

Egypt. Hamas is considering dramatic increases in taxes on cigarettes, gasoline, propane, and other basic commodities, which would dent its popularity. Even Hamas' tunneling infrastructure is at risk now that Egypt—with U.S. help—has begun to crack down on the tunnels, building a barrier along its border with Gaza that extends over 20 meters underground.

Perhaps most damaging to Hamas was its failure to emerge from the 2008-9 Gaza war with the aura of victory that Hezbollah enjoyed after its 2006 war with Israel. Hamas' military strategy was poor, as was its implementation. The Hamas official Mahmoud al- Zahar had warned soon before the war, "Just let them try to invade Gaza. Gaza will be their new Lebanon," but Hamas found itself completely outmatched by the IDF and Israel's intelligence services. No Hamas terrorist cells attacked Israel from the West Bank or within Israel proper, and Israel did not lose one tank or one helicopter or suffer one kidnapping. Hamas' rocket attacks tapered off as the conflict ended rather than growing in intensity, as Hezbollah's had in 2006, which allowed Hezbollah to claim it was unbowed when the guns went silent.

Hamas' political weakness outside Gaza also became evident during Operation Cast Lead. Hamas received no significant support from Arab states: most worried that the Islamist opposition in their own countries would get a boost from a Hamas victory. Even Hezbollah gave only rhetorical support, for fear of renewed conflict with Israel. In the West Bank, Abbas was successful in stopping pro-Hamas demonstrations, using the rebuilt Palestinian police and security services to suppress dissent.

Politically, Hamas is beset from all sides, and its leaders worry that they are losing ground. Fatah is always waiting in the wings, with Abbas salivating over any weakness on the part of Hamas. At the other end of the spectrum, the PIJ hopes it can gain support from disaffected Hamas members by claiming the mantle of Islamic resistance if Hamas moves toward a lasting cease-fire. The extreme Islamist position evokes considerable sympathy among Hamas' rank and file, particularly in the armed wing. In August

2009, Abdel Latif Moussa, a preacher in Gaza whose ideology resembles Osama bin Laden's, declared Gaza an Islamic emirate—a direct challenge to Hamas' caution on this score. Hamas fighters swarmed his mosque, resulting in a shootout that left 28 people dead, including Moussa.

For now at least, Hamas can neither govern freely nor fight effectively, and so it risks losing out to moderates on one side and groups more extreme than itself on the other. Improving the economy in Gaza from abysmal to simply poor would be one victory. So would allowing some Gazans to escape the quarantine the international community has imposed. But to accomplish either of those things, Hamas will have to be willing to make the existing cease-fire more permanent. Doing so would remove the immediate risk of another devastating and embarrassing military operation. Talks with Israel and the rest of the international community, particularly Western officials, would also demonstrate that Hamas is the voice of the Palestinian people in Gaza, and greater legitimacy could bring more aid to Gaza from international organizations and Arab states that so far have shied away from Hamas under international pressure. And if Hamas then managed to govern successfully, it could hope to gain more political power down the road.

Deal or No Deal?

In order for Hamas to want the cease-fire to last, Israel and its allies must change the organization's decision-making calculus—a process that will require both incentives and threats, political and military, and, above all, time.

One way to go about this would be for Israel to make a short-term concession on border crossings, allowing the regular flow of goods into Gaza with international, rather than Israeli, monitors manning the crossing points. Israeli intelligence would still watch what goes in and out to ensure that the international monitors did their job, but symbolically the switch would be important. In exchange, Hamas would commit to a lasting cease-fire and agree to stop all attacks from the territory under its control; in other words, it would no longer allow the PIJ to fight in its stead. Hamas would also close the tunnels and end its smuggling. To make the deal more politically palatable for both sides and remove another bone of contention between them, it should include a prisoner exchange that swaps Shalit for Palestinian prisoners. The deal would not require Hamas to officially recognize Israel or Israel to recognize Hamas (which Hamas does not want anyway).

Egypt would have to broker such an arrangement. Like Israel and the PA, Cairo does not want Hamas to succeed: Hamas emerged from the Muslim Brotherhood movement, Egypt's main opposition force, and its success could have an impact in Egypt itself. At the same time, Cairo wants to separate itself from Gaza; it does not want crises there to further damage its credibility by making it look like an ally of Israel in oppressing Muslims.

Such a deal would allow Hamas to claim credit for improving the lives of Gazans, and it could use the resulting increase in the flow of goods to reward its supporters. Also, Hamas' dealings with additional outside actors could widen the circle of those who tacitly recognize Hamas. For Israel, the regular rocket attacks would come to a complete halt and the threat of renewed attacks would diminish, allowing Israelis living near Gaza to resume their normal lives. Hamas' rockets could rust. A cease-fire would also free up Israel diplomatically. If the problem of Hamas receded, Israel could take more risks in the West Bank and give Palestinians more control over security with less fear that this would lead to a Hamas takeover. Meanwhile, Abbas could negotiate with less fear that Hamas might undermine him. Internationally, a cease-fire would reduce, although hardly eliminate, some of the anger at Israel or at least take Gaza off the front pages.

The hope for Israel is that a long-term cease-fire would, over time, produce its own momentum. Peace would push Hamas to emphasize governance more, strengthen the group's moderates, and discourage its leaders from attacking Israel. Hamas' military capabilities might grow, but it would be reluctant to risk any economic improvements in Gaza in another round of fighting. Hamas could crack down on or neutralize groups such as the PIJ and the Salafi jihadists without risking its popular support. Hamas' ties to Iran would diminish—an important fact for Israel if tension between Tehran and Jerusalem grew over Iran's nuclear program—and indeed Tehran would be bitter that its stalking-horse had turned away from violence. Finally, a cease-fire that allowed goods to flow into Gaza would make it harder for Hamas to blame all of its constituents' problems on Israel.

Hedging Against Failure

Formalizing the cease-fire with Hamas would raise the question of whether Israel and moderate Palestinians were simply postponing an inevitable fight and allowing the enemy to get stronger in the meantime. There is some validity to this concern. Certainly, the growth of Gaza's economy and the increased flow of goods, such as concrete, that can have both civilian and military uses would help Hamas' military. And Hamas has been taking advantage of the current lull in fighting to better arm and train its forces.

With border crossings open, however, Egypt and international monitors could more easily justify completely halting traffic through the tunnels than they can today, since the goods that would be smuggled would exclusively be contraband. Now, stopping the tunnel traffic is too politically sensitive: with both weapons and consumer goods being smuggled in, it would mean exposing Gazans to the risk of starvation. Privately, even some Israelis and Egyptians recognize that some smuggling should be allowed. But if legal trade becomes possible, there will be no more excuse for smuggling. Whatever military advantages Hamas would gain from the freer flow of trade, moreover, would be small: Hamas smuggles so much through the tunnels today that the relative increase in imports that could have military uses would be less than most Israelis fear. In any event, Hamas would still be a pygmy to the Israeli giant.

Another risk of striking a deal with Hamas is that Palestinian moderates would rightly complain that Israel was rewarding violence: once again, their biggest rival would be benefiting from concessions from Israel without having to accept the political price of peace. And if Gaza's economy improved, the contrast between living conditions there and living conditions in the West Bank would become less stark, which would hurt Abbas politically. Thus, in order to offset any political gains Hamas might make, the international community should encourage Fayyad's efforts to provide law and order, reduce corruption, and otherwise start building a state in the West Bank. This would help make the PA a true rival to Hamas when it came to governance.

Fatah would also benefit politically because Hamas could no longer argue against rejecting violence and talking to Israel; however indirectly, it would be doing these things itself. At the same time, Abbas and Fayyad need the political legitimacy that would come with any success in peace negotiations with Israel. If the settlements grow and the talks stagnate, Hamas' argument that what works is resistance, not negotiations, will only gain force. A deal would also place a heavy burden on the PA to outgovern its rival, which is not necessarily a bad thing. An ideal way to move forward would be by reconciling Hamas and Fatah. For Israel, reconciliation would mean that Abbas could cut a deal for all Palestinians and not have it rejected by Hamas. For now, however, that remains unlikely, and neither peace talks with Abbas nor a cease-fire in Gaza should wait for this.

The long-term success of a cease-fire is far from guaranteed. It will depend on the personalities, preferences, and political positions of Hamas' leaders and on the vicissitudes of Israeli politics. The silver lining, however, is that even failure could have its benefits. Right now, Hamas gains from the perception that Israel and the international community seek to crush the Palestinians. Opening the crossings into Gaza would dispel this impression and place Hamas in a difficult spot politically: it would have to give up either on resistance or on governance.

If the rocket attacks from Gaza resumed or if credible evidence emerged that Hamas was dramatically increasing its military capabilities, Israel would have a strong case for resuming the siege or using force. The international community, therefore, must support not only the idea of formalizing the cease-fire but also Israel's right to retaliate militarily in Gaza if, despite Israel's concessions, Hamas resorted to violence. Such backing would both make success in convincing Hamas to adhere to the cease-fire more likely and give Israel a Plan B should the cease-fire collapse. Failure might also foster splits within Hamas. Currently, the group's leaders disagree over how much to emphasize resistance over governance. Making the choice starker may not force Hamas to abandon resistance, but it could steer relative moderates away from the group.

Hamas is here to stay. Refusing to deal with it will only make the situation worse: Palestinian moderates will become weaker, and Hamas will grow stronger. If the Obama administration is to move its plans for peace forward, the challenge of Hamas has to be met first. At stake is not just the failure of the peace process but also the possibility of another war and of Israel occupying Gaza again.

The Palestinian Spring?

Hamas and Fatah Have Unified, but not Yet Reconciled

Robert M. Danin

S oon after the Arab revolts began, thousands of West Bankers
and Gazans took to the streets. Unlike their fellow Arabs,
however, the Palestinians clamored for new unity efforts
rather than new leaders. For their parts, both the Fatah-dominated
Palestinian Authority (PA) in the West Bank and Hamas' de facto
government in Gaza had professed a desire to reunify ever since
they broke apart four years ago. But the enmity and differences
between them had been too great to overcome. As Fatah and
Hamas' patrons fell from power or were severely weakened, Palestinian leaders realized that they would need to renew their legitimacy from within and that unification would be their best bet. For
better or worse, this week's unity agreement between Fatah and
Hamas would never have occurred had the ongoing Arab uprisings
not changed both parties' political fortunes.

Now Palestinians are committed to a dangerous course—many
of the unity agreement's critical details remain either unknown or
unresolved. Although the Palestinians may be on a path toward
political reunification, true reconciliation is unlikely and peace

ROBERT M. DANIN is Eni Enrico Mattei Senior Fellow for Middle East and
Africa Studies at the Council on Foreign Relations. He headed the Jerusalem
mission of Quartet Representative Tony Blair from April 2008 to June 2010
and is a former U.S. Deputy Assistant Secretary of State for Near Eastern Affairs and a former Director for the Levant and Israeli-Palestinian Affairs at the
National Security Council.

negotiations with Israel are now off the table for the foreseeable future. A United Nations vote granting Palestine membership in the General Assembly this September would only complicate matters. It could lead to unilateral Israeli actions on the ground and renewed Israeli-Palestinian violence.

When the Arab uprisings first started in Tunisia last December, Palestinian politics were already in tumult. Negotiations with Israel over the establishment of a Palestinian state were stalemated with no prospect of renewal in sight. Meanwhile, Hamas had been pummeling Mahmoud Abbas, leader of the Palestinian Liberation Organization, the umbrella group recognized by Israel and most of the world as the representative of the Palestinian people, and the PA over Al Jazeera's January 24 publication of some 1600 leaked internal documents, which portrayed Palestinian peace negotiators as having been overly accommodating towards Israel after the 2008 Annapolis peace conference without gaining much in return.

In the days that followed, the lead Palestinian negotiator, Saeb Erekat, tendered his resignation. In the West Bank, PA leaders who had long sought peace with Israel as a path toward nationhood hardened their terms for resuming the peace talks. Demonstrators there denounced Qatar and Al Jazeera for interfering in Palestinian affairs. Meanwhile, in Gaza, Hamas-sponsored protesters denounced the PA for its purported willingness to make fundamental concessions, especially over Jerusalem and Palestinian refugees.

In February, Egyptian President Hosni Mubarak's ouster came as a shock, especially to Abbas. Throughout his rule, Mubarak had helped maintain the legitimacy of the PA's quest for negotiated peace with Israel by adhering to the Egyptian-Israeli peace treaty and also claiming an active role in inter-Arab politics. Mubarak had also provided a line of communication between Abbas and Israel's leaders and had given Abbas political mentorship.

Now, with Israeli-Palestinian negotiations stalled, unrest raging throughout the Arab world, and Mubarak's political cover lost, Palestinian leaders tried to shift the national agenda from peace with Israel toward reestablishing legitimacy and unity at home, lest the calls for regime change infect Palestinian territory. In February, Abbas called on Prime Minister Salam Fayyad, an independent, to disband the PA government and reshuffle the cabinet. Meanwhile, the Fatah-dominated PLO called for municipal elections across the West Bank and Gaza in July, and presidential and legislative elections no later than September.

For Hamas, Mubarak's fall was a godsend. Gone, along with Mubarak, was his intelligence chief Omar Suleiman, whose hostility towards Hamas was barely veiled. Both men had routinely pressed Hamas to make concessions to Fatah. Frequently, they had closed the Rafah border crossing between Egypt and Gaza to keep Hamas effectively sealed off from its ideological brethren, the banned Egyptian Muslim Brotherhood. With Mubarak and Suleiman now gone, the Muslim Brotherhood back in the fore, and Cairo pursuing a new "independent" foreign policy, Egypt was no longer as closely aligned with Washington and far less hostile to Hamas. Indeed, just after Mubarak's ouster, Egypt's new government started talking about reopening the Rafah border crossing.

When tens of thousands of Gazans took to the streets to call for reconciliation with the West Bank, Hamas used violence to suppress them. The organization continued to reject Abbas' call for a new unity government of independents, clinging to its demand for the formation of an interim government, which would be comprised in part by Hamas members.

Despite popular protests in Gaza, Hamas appeared to be on the ascendance until the Arab revolt spread to Syria. Hamas' avowed neutrality between the Syrian government and the protesters strained ties between Assad and the Hamas leadership, much of which is based in Damascus. Unsure how much longer its Syrian base would last, Hamas agreed to fundamental concessions that made unity possible. In secret negotiations brokered by Egypt, Hamas dropped its longstanding insistence on its participation in the new caretaker government. On May 4th, Hamas leader Khaled Mashaas and Abbas signed the unity accord.

Most Palestinians were surprised when the agreement was announced. It creates a neutral caretaker government to oversee the transition to an elected PA president, parliament, and PLO National Council. The government that manages this transition will not be empowered to advance the peace process with Israel, nor will it be structured to pursue Palestinian statehood—those tasks will be left to whomever wins the elections. But by ostensibly bringing together the rival factions, the agreement at least represents an attempt at enhanced legitimacy and an opportunity to further the state-building process.

Still, it papers over many key differences between Fatah and Hamas, including disagreements over how security services should be managed and the future political platform of the PLO. Uncertainty also remains about whether Fayyad will head the new government. A leading proponent of reform, Fayyad had been among first to call for reconciliation once the Arab uprising first broke out. His focus on financial probity and security has antagonized both Fatah and Hamas, who seek more latitude for their own parochial interests. Both parties would prefer to see a less powerful figure that Fayyad assume leadership.

Although there have been some reports that Fayyad will not be considered to head the new government, he is, in fact, not out of the running. His solid international reputation is the Palestinian's best hope for continued Western assistance and for the continuation of efforts to strengthen Palestinian institutions and the private sector. If a Hamas-led government took power, aid would surely be cut off and Palestinian nationbuilding would stagnate.

Perhaps the greatest challenge after the interim government takes over will be holding fair elections and creating a representative government while preventing Hamas from usurping the process. For years, the PA and the PLO have accepted mutual Israeli- Palestinian recognition and the peaceful resolution of outstanding conflicts as key tenets of Palestinian politics. But Hamas has always rejected these ideas. Should Hamas continue to refuse to recognize Israel and commit to non-violence, the Palestinian national movement will either split once again, or will have come full circle to its position in the 1960s, that violent resistance and rejectionism are the means for achieving Palestinian aspirations. As has recently been the case, the ongoing Arab Spring will shape the decisions all Palestinians take in the period ahead.

Israel's Gamble in Gaza

Daniel Byman

Israel's latest campaign in Gaza, which began on Wednesday with the killing of Hamas' military commander, Ahmed Jabari, and air strikes on the group's long-range rocket launchers, is a gamble—and one that Israel might lose. Its goal is to compel Hamas to stop shooting rockets into Israel from the Gaza Strip and to crack down on other groups who are also doing so. Hamas, however, will find it hard to bend to Israeli pressure. In turn, it will be up to outside states, particularly Egypt, to foster a deal to end the fighting.

After Operation Cast Lead, the Israeli incursion into Gaza in 2008-2009 that resulted in over 1,000 Palestinian deaths and tremendous destruction, relations between Hamas and Israel wavered uneasily between hostility and tacit cooperation. True, Hamas' rhetoric toward Israel remained hostile, but the number of rockets that went over the border plunged and most of them were launched not by Hamas, but by more radical groups such as Palestinian Islamic Jihad. Hamas feared that launching large numbers of rockets would prompt Israel to again retaliate harshly and devastate Gaza, thus jeopardizing Hamas' political position there. At times, the group even tried to restrain its uncomfortable bedfellows. Indeed, although Hamas and Israel would both deny it, their interests were often aligned. As Aluf Benn, one of Israel's leading analysts, put it after Jabari's death, "Ahmed Jabari was a subcontractor, in charge of maintaining Israel's security in Gaza."

DANIEL BYMAN is a professor in the Security Studies Program in the School of Foreign Service at Georgetown University and the research director of the Saban Center at Brookings. He is the author of *A High Price: The Triumph and Failures of Israeli Counterterrorism*.

But Jabari's first allegiance, of course, was to Hamas. And, over time, Hamas became increasingly accepting of attacks on Israel. As the memory of Cast Lead faded, the number of attacks coming from Gaza began to rise once more. Israel claims that over

200 rockets struck the country in 2010. The number climbed to over 600 in 2011. And 2012 has seen even more—over 800 before the current operation began. Most of these attacks came from other Palestinian groups, but more recently Hamas seemed to take a more active role in the violence, openly tolerating other groups' gambits and carrying out some strikes itself.

By this week, those attacks had "made normal life impossible for over one million Israelis," as Israeli Prime Minister Benjamin Netanyahu explained on Thursday. And so he and his government are again pounding Hamas in an attempt to restore the post- Cast Lead status quo, in which Hamas polices both itself and the rest of the strip. So far, Operation Pillar of Defense, as Israel calls it, has resulted in the deaths of 18 Palestinians (of whom roughly half were civilians). Hamas' response has killed three Israelis.

No single attack forced Israel to respond. In theory, it could have chosen not to. But the steady increase in rocket fire over the last few years had become politically intolerable for the Netanyahu government. With national elections approaching in January, his administration seemed unable to carry out perhaps government's most basic function: protecting citizens from violence. In addition, although Israel's political and security leaders might recognize the difference, ordinary Israelis simply did not care whether Hamas launched attacks itself or simply did not stop others from doing so. In other words, it was time to take out Hamas or else risk being taken out of office.

By launching this operation, Israel has resorted to its time-honored strategy of holding the government (or in Hamas' case, de facto government) that hosts militants responsible for the actions of the militants themselves. The approach has had some successes: in Jordan in 1970, Israel pressured Amman to instigate a bloody civil war against the country's Palestinian militants, eventually

Daniel Byman

crushing them. But in Lebanon later in the same decade, Israel tried the same thing, with much worse results. The Lebanese government was too weak to crack down on terrorist activity in its borders and the country descended into chaos. In 2006, the same logic drove Israel's war against Hezbollah in Lebanon. Although the war was initially seen widely as a Hezbollah victory, Israelis now see it as a win. The Israeli military performed poorly, but Hezbollah has grudgingly kept the peace since then, fearing that rocket attacks from Lebanon would again lead to a devastating Israeli response. Indeed, the last six years have been the quietest along the Lebanon-Israel border in decades.

Israel's usual strategy might not bring about such decisive results this time. Hamas will find it hard to pull itself back from the brink and start stopping others' rocket fire. Jabari's death has infuriated Hamas' military wing, and whoever replaces him will be just as militant, if not more. Such a leader will press for revenge and warn Hamas' governing arm that his troops might well join rival groups if Hamas throws in the towel. After all, Hamas is trying to be both a resistance movement and a government. In many ways, it has succeeded as a government, establishing law and order and delivering basic services in Gaza. But Hamas must take care not to lose credibility among Palestinians for its willingness to fight—and die—in the struggle against Israel. So Hamas has tried to walk a fine line by allowing some attacks—and, at times, even participating in them—to maintain its militant street cred while shying away from an all-out assault that would push Israel to repeat Cast Lead.

Complicating the Israel-Hamas dynamic is the Arab Spring, particularly the fall of President Hosni Mubarak and the rise of Egypt's Muslim Brotherhood-led government. During the Mubarak era, Egypt helped Israel contain Hamas, maintaining a blockade on goods from Gaza and a travel ban on Gazans as well as supporting Hamas' rival, Fatah. During crises, Cairo often worked with Israel to press Hamas to back off. Today, however, Hamas has an ideological affinity with, and personal ties to, to the government of Egypt's new president, Mohammad Morsi. Meanwhile, the

Muslim Brotherhood wants to court the Egyptian public, which is viscerally anti-Israel and highly supportive of Hamas. Openly siding with Israel in this conflict would be political suicide for Morsi. So, not surprisingly, Egypt has recalled its ambassador from Israel and publicly criticized Israel.

Israel, too, cannot afford to alienate Egypt. Putting aside the vital 1979 Egyptian-Israeli peace treaty (which still seems likely to hold), Jerusalem needs Cairo to keep whatever little pressure it can on Hamas. Although the rhetoric between the Morsi government and Hamas is far warmer than it was under Mubarak, the new government in Cairo has still not rushed to open up the Rafah border crossing with Gaza. In addition, Israel needs the Egyptian government to continue, and ideally expand, its recent crackdown on radicals in the Sinai, who have repeatedly attacked Israel. Finally, Israel needs the Egyptian government to refrain from whipping up pro-Hamas sentiment among its own people, which could quickly spread across the region and further destabilize already vulnerable countries like Jordan.

Israel also lacks any easy option to escalate if Hamas does not restrain itself soon. Although Israel has called up reservists and threatened to expand the scope of its military campaign if Hamas doesn't end the rocket attacks, Israelis do not want to reoccupy Gaza. What is more, the Obama administration would be unlikely to get behind a massive operation, since it would further complicate already tense U.S. relations with Egypt and other Arab countries. Perhaps most important, Israel's view of itself would be in danger. The western way of war stresses proportionality, which, in Gaza, means that Israel must limit its strikes—particularly on infrastructure and other targets that directly affect civilians. The logic of deterrence, by contrast, stresses disproportionate punishment: the enemy must suffer.

In the short run, the United States should press the Morsi government to broker a deal: a development that would not only end the current crisis but also indicate that Morsi can be a responsible leader who can work with Washington. In the long run, the United

States, and the world, needs to make the choice between resistance and governance sharper for Hamas. There must be more and real rewards if Hamas moves toward becoming a regular government that eschews violence. Allowing more normal economic activity and more people to go to and from Gaza would show Hamas that the world will let it govern Gaza. At the same time, there must be serious and sustained punishment for any continued rocket attacks or other violence with the international community maintaining economic pressure on Hamas and accepting that Israel will hit Hamas hard to keep its deterrence credible. But Cast Lead showed that any military campaign, no matter how devastating, can only deter Israel's enemies for so long. Israel and the international community need to take some bold political risks in trying to bring Hamas into the fold—or else start preparing for the next war.

Hamas' Miscalculation

Why the Group Thought it Could Get Away With Striking Israel

Barak Mendelsohn

The escalation in the fighting last week between Israel and Hamas caught many observers by surprise. Operation Cast Lead, Israel's 2008 campaign against Hamas, had led to an uneasy calm between the warring sides. And last year's release of Gilad Shalit (the Israeli soldier who had been kidnapped by militants in 2006) in exchange for a thousand Palestinian prisoners had even given observers hope that Israel and Hamas had found a way to manage their conflict. But then, Hamas attacked an Israeli mobile patrol inside Israeli territory on November 10 and Israel retaliated by assassinating Ahmed Jabari, Hamas's military chief. This time, the violence that has followed has not faded quickly; indeed, the fight is still intensifying.

Given the destruction wrought by Israel and Hamas' last major conflict, Hamas' calculations in the lead-up to this round of fighting are especially puzzling. The typical explanation is that Hamas ramped up its rocket campaign earlier this year in an effort to break Israel's siege on the Gaza Strip. Under fire, Israel had to retaliate.

That answer, though, is unsatisfying. In many ways, the siege had already been broken. True, the Gaza Strip is tiny, densely populated, squeezed between Israel and Egypt, and dependent on both

BARAK MENDELSOHN is Assistant Professor of Political Science at Haverford College and the author of *Combating Jihadism: American Hegemony and Interstate Cooperation in the War on Terrorism*.

countries for the passage of people and goods. And all of that makes it a rather claustrophobic place. Yet Israel's efforts to tightly control the area's borders, which started after Hamas won elections there in 2006, had gradually wound down. After the public relations disaster that followed Israel's 2010 mishandling of the Gaza-bound Turkish aid flotilla, the flow of goods over the Israeli border into Gaza increased substantially. Moreover, the tunnels under the Egypt-Gaza border, through which most of the goods coming into Gaza are smuggled, became so elaborate that they resembled official border crossings. In fact, the volume of trade that travels through the tunnels could be up to $700 million dollars a year.

To some extent, Hamas had a political interest in perpetuating the siege idea, which could be used to foment anger against Israel and drum up popular support. Further, it made sense for the movement to preserve some limitations on the movement of goods into Gaza, since the smuggling industry lined its coffers. Thus, although life in Gaza might not have been all that pleasant for Gazans, Hamas wanting to break the siege is not a compelling explanation for its renewed violence against Israel.

In fact, two factors pushed Hamas to ramp up its bombing campaign: competition from Salafi groups and Hamas' belief that its strategic environment had improved in the wake of the Arab Spring. Since Hamas was elected, it has found the Salafi groups in Gaza especially difficult rivals to manage. Fatah, Hamas' main competitor before it pushed the group out of the area in 2006, was never such a challenge: with the Oslo peace process discredited and Israel's retreat from the Gaza Strip largely attributed (at least in the Gazan psychology) to Hamas' militant activities, the remnants of Fatah just couldn't compete. The small jihadi outfits, though, embodied the fighting ethos. And unlike Hamas, they were free from the constraints that governing puts on ideological purity.

Under pressure, Hamas repeatedly tried to quell the Salafi threat, and it did not shy from using brute force to do so. The clearest demonstration came in August 2009, when Hamas killed the leader of Jund Ansar Allah, a Salafi group that had openly challenged Hamas' authority, and a number of its members. But short of using extreme violence to suppress Salafism in Gaza, which would have been too costly for Hamas, Hamas could not eliminate the Salafi challenge. It watched with worry as new Salafi groups emerged and strengthened throughout the strip.

The pressure on Hamas only increased in the wake of the 2011 Arab uprisings. The Egyptian revolution and the subsequent chaos in the Sinai Peninsula were a backwind in the sails of Gaza's Salafis. The collapse of authoritarian regimes in North Africa unleashed a flood of weapons and fighters, which Salafis channeled into the Sinai Peninsula. With the Egyptian military unable to control the area, Gazan Salafis turned the peninsula into a staging ground for attacking Israel. They believed (correctly) that Israel, anxious not to kill its peace accord with Egypt, would not dare to respond directly.

Indeed, Israel resorted to thwarting attacks emerging from Sinai and the Gaza Strip as best it could by preventing Gazans from getting to Sinai in the first place. On a number of occasions, Israel preemptively targeted Salafi leaders in Gaza. The Salafis responded by lobbing rockets back at Israeli's southern towns. Periods of quiet between rounds of violence became shorter and rarer.

The new regional order presented Hamas with a serious dilemma. As the ruler of Gaza, it could not sit on the sidelines while Israel targeted territory under its control. But it was unable to fully rein in the Salafis without proving once and for all that it was no longer a resistance movement. For Hamas, then, the only choice was to tolerate the attacks. It portrayed them at home as a way to preserve the struggle against Israel. Abroad, it refused to acknowledge any role in them at all to reduce the danger of a backlash. Over time, pressure from Hamas rank and file led the organization to take a more active role in each round of violence.

The flaw in Hamas' logic, though, was that it assumed that Israel would cooperate and not retaliate. Israel would not let Hamas shirk responsibility, though, and demanded that Hamas assert its authority over the radical factions. To reinforce the message, this year, Israel carried out a number of strikes on Hamas targets. Once it became a target itself, Hamas was even less able able to show restraint. It eventually resumed carrying out its own strikes on Israel, a move that was cheered by the Hamas rank and file, who, without such attacks, might have defected to the more radical groups.

Another of Hamas' miscalculations was expecting Egypt to be supportive of its actions, which, when combined with Israel's fear of alienating the regime in Cairo, would allow Hamas to escalate the conflict without it spinning out of control. The hope was not off base. In August, Egyptian President Mohamed Morsi had retired the military's top brass and taken full control of Egypt's foreign and security police. The development was particularly significant given that the Supreme Military Council, which had maintained close relations with the United States, was not as interested in helping Hamas. But, the group was wrong again. Hamas' closer ties with Egypt did not discourage Israel from fighting back.

Simply put, Hamas' strategic environment was not as favorable as it thought. When it tried to push Israel's boundaries, Israel pushed back. Now the group is in a bind. It needs a face-saving resolution to the fighting, one that would allow it to claim some achievement worth of the devastation inflicted this month on Gaza. Even after that, the group will still face the same old tension between its ideology of resistance and the responsibilities that come with governing. And all the while, its Salafi challengers will be lurking, challenging its commitment to the struggle against Israel. If Hamas wants to avoid future such escalations, it will need to crack down on these groups. But that would come with a price—in popularity and legitimacy—that Hamas seems unwilling to pay. Hamas must also finally make the transition from resistance movement to normal political party. It will probably take a push from Cairo for that to happen. Hamas' alliance with Egypt's Muslim Brotherhood offers the group some of the cover it needs to make the much-needed transition. And the Muslim Brotherhood is a good model for Hamas to follow, besides. Absent Hamas' political transformation, no cease-fire with Israel will hold for long. The next round of violence awaits, just over the horizon.

Where Hamas Goes From Here

Time To Regroup or Rupture

Thanassis Cambanis

O nce again, Hamas has been spared from making the difficult political choice that faces most resistance movements
when they gain power: whether to focus on the fight or to
govern. Since it won the Palestinian elections in 2006 and then
took control of the Gaza Strip in 2007, Hamas has been free to
pursue a middle course, resisting Israel while blaming its political
failures on its cold war with Fatah and on Israel's blockade. Now
Hamas will tout the concessions it won from Israel last week—
as part of the ceasefire, Israel agreed to open the border crossings
to Gaza, suspend its military operations there, and end targeted
killings—as proof that it should not give up fighting. Meanwhile,
the outcome should be enough to buy Hamas cover for its poor
record of governance and allow it to again defer making tough
choices about statehood, negotiations, regional alliances, and military strategy. The group might even be able to use the momentum
to supplant Fatah in the West Bank as it has done in Gaza.

Hamas' recent advance won't fully mask the organization's central dilemma, nor will it cover internal rifts about how to solve it.
In the American and Israeli media, portrayals of Hamas often focus heavily on the group's commitment to eliminating the Jewish

THANASSIS CAMBANIS is a fellow at the Century Foundation. He is a foreign
policy columnist for The Boston Globe, and he blogs at thanassiscambanis.com.

state. And certainly any fair study of the group should take into account that goal. Yet for Hamas, the end of Israel is more an ideological starting point than a practical program. And what comes after the starting point is unclear: Hamas has never developed a vision of what a resolution short of total victory might look like, nor has it spelled out an agenda for governing its own constituents, despite all these years in power. In part, that is because Hamas is a diffuse and contested movement, whose competing factions all work toward their own self-interest.

Hamas' top political leadership used to operate out of Damascus but scattered to Cairo, Doha, and other Middle Eastern capitals this year as Syria descended into chaos. Since then, the exiled leadership has clashed publicly with Hamas' Gaza-based leadership. Khaled Meshal, the organization's main leader, now based Doha, and his cohort have generally allied with the Sunni Arab states over Iran, welcoming the rise of Islamists in Egypt, in Tunisia, and among the Syrian rebels. Meshal himself has publicly endorsed a truce with Israel based on Israel's withdrawal to its 1967 borders. The rest of the exile- based leaders have also indicated their willingness to consider a truce, although they say they would consider the deal temporary and would not recognize Israel. Partly in response to Hamas' pragmatism, and partly in acceptance of the reality of the movement's rising power, Arab leaders finally ended their informal boycott of Gaza. In recent months, the emir of Qatar and the prime minister of Egypt paid visits.

Yet the growing stature of Hamas might accentuate, rather than diffuse, the tensions between its exiled chiefs and its Gaza-based leadership. According to Mark Perry, a historian who follows Palestinian politics, Hamas' prime minister, Ismail Haniya, has endorsed a close relationship with Iran. For his part, Haniya paid a warm visit to Tehran in February, provoking the ire of Arab leaders, who have since given him the cold shoulder, preferring instead to meet with other Hamas leaders. Haniya has expressed no interest in talking about a two state solution and overall, the rest of the Gaza-based leadership has simply grown more uncompromising under the Israeli blockade and now two lopsided wars. It prefers full-throated resistance to any political settlement.

It is unclear whether the differences presage an ideological split or are simply the result of two very different vantage points: inside Gaza, where the leaders have to worry about staying in power, and outside it, where the leaders worry about staying regionally relevant. So far, Hamas has seemed unable to address the issues that divide the two factions, which might explain why the movement has not selected a successor to Meshal, who was supposed to step down this spring. The sides do, of course, have lowest common denominators that hold them together: resistance as the primary avenue to winning Palestinian rights; gaining greater share of Palestinian leadership; and Islamism.

Since Hamas' creation in 1987, it has tried to match Fatah's strength. With that goal largely accomplished by 2007, it has moved on to pushing Fatah completely to the sidelines by maintaining a commitment to Islamism and opposition to the Jewish state. By contrast, Fatah has remained secular, and has even agreed to recognize Israel and to conduct an experiment in joint governance with it through the Palestinian Authority. Two decades into the Oslo process, Fatah has little to show for its efforts. Meanwhile, Hamas has not had to face Palestinian voters since 2006. Polling suggests that Palestinians—Gazans in particular—have lost patience with Hamas. But each conflict with Israel gives the movement a new lease on life.

As recently as last week, Israel was describing in breathless terms the latest tepid exploits of the smoky, aging leader of Fatah, Mahmoud Abbas, who is on the verge of obtaining non-member observer status at the United Nations. Israel's foreign ministry was reportedly circulating policy options to deal with his gambit that included dismantling the Palestinian Authority and withholding its rightful tax revenues, which would effectively subject the West Bank to the same kind of isolation that Gaza has faced since Hamas took power. That would play directly to the long-term goals shared by Hamas' leaders in Gaza as well as those in exile: to take over from Fatah the role of primary representative of all Palestinians.

What is more, developments in the region have boosted Hamas' position. This is not the Middle East of the last war, in 2008-09, when, for the most part, the Arab world stood by as Israel subjected Gaza to overwhelming and disproportionate bombing. That conflict killed 1,387 Palestinians and 13 Israelis. Hosni Mubarak's government in Cairo even assisted the Israeli campaign against Hamas, while the West and Arab world poured money into Fatah's West Bank government as a counterweight to Hamas. The regional landscape now is entirely different. Still, despite a warm rhetorical embrace for Hamas, the Egyptian state has yet to significantly change its policy. It hasn't opened the border with Gaza, nor does it want to do anything that would allow Israel to shift responsibility for Gaza to Egypt. Throughout the cease-fire negotiations, Israel said Egypt would be responsible for keeping the peace. But no matter what Israel says now, the language of the agreement and the reality on the ground make clear that Israel struck a deal with Hamas at Egypt's insistence, and that Egypt will certainly be no guarantor of Hamas' behavior. That's an achievement for the ruling Muslim Brotherhood. As its (and Egypt's) influence grows, it might be able to promote its preferred exiled Hamas leaders at the expense of the more uncompromising ones in Gaza.

Hamas has other competitors to worry about now. Until the uprisings two years ago, the Middle East's Islamist movements were mostly on the outside looking in, railing against secular nationalist despots. In fact, Hamas and Hezbollah were the only Islamist movements who could claim to have ascended to power through popular victories at the ballot box. In the pre-uprising Arab world, then, Hamas (like Hezbollah) could plausibly claim some leadership of a regional Islamist movement. No more. The Muslim Brotherhood now governs Egypt. Islamists were elected to power in Tunisia. They have also emerged as power centers in Libya and among the Syrian opposition. Now that Islamists are competing for power in large states, Hamas (and Hezbollah) could shrink to their proper size in terms of influence. This outcome seems even more likely now that Hamas faces a vibrant challenge from jihadi fundamentalists within Gaza who consider Hamas far too moderate.

Hamas has presented itself as a voice for resistance, but as Gaza tries to rebuild and recover from this latest war, the organization will have to grapple with its own authoritarian, corrupt record in power. Its exiled leaders might sound more reasonable to Western ears, but they're not the ones who actually control territory and manage a government. If it gets what it wants—a central role in Palestinian leadership—Hamas will have to reconcile its own internal factions or else risk a split. On the quickly changing ground of the new Arab politics, Hamas, like other governing movements, will have to articulate an ever-more detailed, constructive program, to convince rather than compel its constituents.

Hamas' Not-So-Secret Weapon

Meet Salah al-Arouri, the Man Behind the Group's Kidnapping Strategy

Matthew Levitt

S oon after three Israel teenagers were kidnapped last month, Israeli officials leaked to the press the name of the Hamas operational commander who is believed to be behind a recent surge in kidnapping plots. It was a familiar one for those who follow Hamas closely: Salah al-Arouri, a longtime Hamas operative from the West Bank, who lives openly in Turkey. Now, with the boys' bodies found and the funerals over, Israeli security forces continue to hunt down the two Hebron-based Hamas operatives believed to have actually carried out the plot. Yet observers and experts are sure to eventually circle back to Arouri, who has been a key figure behind Hamas' efforts to rejuvenate the group's terrorist networks in the West Bank.

In the Beginning

In 2012, Amnesty International described Arouri as "widely held to be one of the founders of the armed wing of Hamas." In court

MATTHEW LEVITT is the Fromer-Wexler fellow and Director of the Stein Program on Counterterrorism at the Washington Institute for Near East Policy. He is the author of *Hamas: Politics, Charity and Terrorism in the Service of Jihad* and *Hezbollah: The Global Footprint of Lebanon's Party of God.*

documents, the U.S. Department of Justice has likewise described him as "a high-ranking Hamas military leader dating back to his role as a Hamas student cell leader at Hebron University in the early 1990s," where he was recruited.

Arouri's time at Hebron University is well documented. In 1985, he started studying sharia law there. By the following year, was elected head of the Islamic Faction at the university. These Islamic Blocs (Kutla Islamiya), which are Hamas' on-campus youth wings, have long been a critical component of Hamas' social and political infrastructure on college campuses, and it was through Arouri's association with them that he met Muin Shabib, a Hamas operative who headed one at Bir Zeit University, right around the time of the founding of Hamas in 1988. Focused on organizing events and sermons for two years, Arouri and Shabib planned to recruit operatives for a Hamas cell, but these early plots were disrupted by Arouri's arrest by Israel in November 1990. Released from prison in April 1991, Arouri picked up where he left off planning terrorist operations.

Arouri recounted a meeting shortly after his release from prison at which "Muayn told me that there was authorization for military activity and gave me a code word for an anonymous person that would come to him, which was 'Abu Hani sends you his regards and wants to make a license.'" When the unnamed man arrived in July or August 1991, Arouri continued, he made contact at the university. "He came to the University in Hebron and gave me the code word," Arouri recalled, and then assigned Arouri "to recruit a squad in Hebron and to obtain weapons."

Arouri would later admit to receiving "approximately $96,000 to procure weapons from Abu Ahmed [Salah] in August 1992" and providing "$45,000 to [Hamas operative] Musa Muhammed Salah Dudin to be used for weapons to conduct attacks." For his part, Dudin—a Hebron University student and Hamas operative who was involved in the murder of an Israeli soldier, Yuval Tutange, in December of 1992—purchased several weapons and used them in several attacks on Israelis. In addition to passing money, Arouri also found himself sheltering wanted Hamas terrorists and smuggling them out of the West Bank, providing weapons to senior Hamas operatives like Imad Aqel, and more. Together with Salah, he played a central role in the resuscitation of Hamas' Qassam brigades in the West Bank. And then he was arrested by Israeli authorities in 1992.

By then—with most of Hamas' military leadership deported outs of the West Bank—Arouri had become a central player in Hamas' efforts to rebuild its terrorist cell networks. According to court documents, he admitted to interrogators that he was responsible for recruiting a cell to carry out attacks, to providing operatives funds received from abroad, and for purchasing weapons. As a direct connection between the West Bank cells that he built and Hamas's U.S.-based financiers, moreover, Arouri played a critical intermediary role between otherwise compartmented elements of Hamas's external leadership and on-the-ground operatives.

Jail Bait

When Arouri was arrested the first time, he spent six months in prison, during which time he met other Hamas operatives and discussed notional military plans. Little did he realize when he was arrested for the second time that he would spend the next 15 years in prison. First held in administrative detention, Arouri was interrogated at length in early 1993 and described in detail what he had been doing in the previous years. Based on this information, he was charged, tried, and convicted to five years in jail for "his leadership role in the Hamas movement."

But before his scheduled release in 1997, Israeli judges approved two six-month renewals of his detention. New charges were then filed against Arouri for "conducting unlawful activities" from inside the prison and making "illegal contact" in individuals outside the prison. According to the U.S. Justice Department, in October 1999, Mohammed Salah sent a Hamas operative to scout Jerusalem locations for Hamas attacks, convey messages to various Hamas operatives, and meet Arouri in prison and to provide funds to his family.

In prison, Arouri retained influence within group's jailed leadership. In 2009, he was elected, along with several other Hamas militants, to head one of the councils of the prison branch of the Majlis al-Shura, Hamas' overarching political and decision-making body in Damascus. He was ultimately released in March 2007, just as Hamas entered a coalition government with Fatah. He got married, gave an interview indicating that he now shunned terror tactics, and seemed resolved to the fact that, as he put it, "Israel is a reality, but not a legitimate reality." But three months later he was arrested by Israeli officials once more. He was held until March 2010, when he was released and warned that if he did not leave the country within several days he would be rearrested. After Jordanian authorities denied his request to enter the country with his wife, Arouri left for Syria, where the external leadership of Hamas was then based. But with the outbreak of violence in Syria, and the breakdown of Hamas' relationships with Syria and Iran over its refusal to back the Assad regime in its crackdown on fellow Sunnis, Arouri moved to Turkey, where he now resides.

New Ideas

Drawing on his past operational experience, an Israeli official told *The Times of Israel*, Arouri "has urged West Bank operatives incessantly to set up terror cells and perpetrate kidnappings." He "financially sponsored these cells, which were trained and directed to abduct Israelis," often sending funds via charities serving as front organizations. Odds are, though, that Israeli authorities won't soon release evidence to back up any off-the-record charges that Arouri was tied to the three teens' kidnapping and murder. In the words of former Israeli National Security Adviser Yaakov Amidror, "Anyone who knows something about Arouri will not tell you, because it's intelligence that should not be published and is needed for the future." Arouri's role overseeing Hamas West Bank operations overall, however—whatever role he did or did not play in this particular plot—is not in dispute.

Nevertheless, over the past couple of years, dozens of operatives dispatched by Arouri tried to enter the West Bank via Jordan with messages directing operatives to carry out kidnappings and funds to finance the operations. Some were identified and arrested, but others gained entry, carried out their assignments, and departed. Consider, for example, the case of Mahmoud Sawalah, arrested in February 2013, who admitted traveling to Jordan for the purpose of receiving funds that he would then deliver to Hamas in the West Bank. Sawalah met terrorist operatives representing several groups in Jordan, mostly Hamas, and admitted that he was also supposed to have received funds from Arouri as well. He and his brother, Ahmed, who was arrested two weeks earlier, attempted to smuggle around 10,000 euros and 900 dollars into the West Bank, hidden in cigarette cartons.

For Hamas, kidnapping plots are especially attractive as a means of targeting Israel while undermining the political standing of the Palestinian Authority, especially when popular support for more spectacular operations like suicide bombings is low. Kidnappings are seen as uniquely legitimate within Palestinian society, which considers the tactic a valid way to press for the release of Palestinian militants imprisoned in Israeli jails. As a Hamas spokesman said 20 years ago when Hamas kidnapped another American-Israeli dual national, Nachshon Wachsman, "The kidnapping is not an end; it is a means for the release of all our prisoners." And whereas Palestinian Authority efforts to secure prisoners' release through negotiations have failed, Hamas officials maintain, kidnappings work. Indeed, Israel has released many jailed militants—many convicted of heinous crimes—for kidnapped Israelis such as Gilad Shalit and even for the bodies of dead Israelis held by groups such as Hamas or Hezbollah.

Arouri's intimate familiarity with the West Bank—he lived near Ramallah, attended college further south in Hebron, and worked with Muin Shabib to the north near Nablus—makes him uniquely suited to overseeing Hamas operations there, and for pursuing the strategy of kidnapping. Moreover, Arouri knows better than most what is required to reconstitute Hamas' covert, operational infrastructure across the West Bank in the face of a security crackdown, since he's done it before. Now, as then, Hamas depends on the support and guidance of Hamas' external leadership. Back then, Hamas relied on the funding and support of key operatives in the United States, such as Mousa Abu Marzouk and Mohammad Salah. Today, Hamas needs similar external support, and it is coming, at least in part, from Arouri in Turkey.

Expendable Egypt

Why Cairo Can't Broker a Ceasefire Between Israel and Hamas

Benedetta Berti and Zack Gold

The similarities between this month's hostilities between Hamas and Israel and those during their last major confrontation, in November 2012, are striking. Hamas and other Palestinian groups fire rockets deep into Israel, and the Iron Dome defense system knocks the projectiles out of the sky. Israel launches aerial strikes on densely populated areas of the Gaza Strip, and militants there shoot rockets back at Israeli civilians.

Yet one thing has changed: the relationship between Hamas and Egypt. In the fall of 2012, Hamas was able to count on the political support of the Egyptian government of President Mohamed Morsi, a Muslim Brotherhood leader. The rise of the Brotherhood in Egypt earlier that year had simultaneously provided Hamas with a new regional ally and redefined relations between the group and Egypt, moving from the mutual deep- seated suspicion and antagonism of the Mubarak years to a relationship built on shared political ideals and respect.

BENEDETTA BERTI is a Postdoctoral Fellow at Ben-Gurion University, a Research Fellow at the Institute for National Security Studies, a lecturer at Tel Aviv University, and the author of Armed Political Organizations. Follow her on Twitter @benedettabertiw.

ZACK GOLD is an Adjunct Fellow at the American Security Project and author of the Brookings Institution's Saban Center analysis paper "Sinai Security: Opportunities for Unlikely Cooperation Among Egypt, Israel, and Hamas." Follow him on Twitter @ZLGold.

After Morsi was ousted in July 2013, the new Egyptian government launched a crackdown on the Brotherhood at home and assumed an especially harsh posture toward Hamas, calling the group, which was once a branch of the Muslim Brotherhood in Gaza, a threat to national security. Most significantly, Egypt's repeated restrictions on the flows of goods and people to and from Gaza and its campaign to crack down on underground tunnels between the strip and Sinai have deeply hurt Hamas's finances. In March 2014, moreover, Egypt's judiciary banned Hamas from conducting any political activities in the country.

Unsurprisingly, Hamas felt the loss of Egypt's political friendship very deeply. Now that it was regionally isolated, internal divisions arose over how to confront the new challenges, with discussions about rekindling relations with Iran as well as about the group's balance between governance and resistance. Hamas's troubles also led competing armed factions to challenge the group's monopoly of force in Gaza, for example by engaging in uncoordinated rocket attacks against Israel. The group also faced a significant cash-flow problem. All together, these pressures arguably pushed Hamas to enter a unity deal with the Fatah movement that controls the West Bank–based Palestinian Authority. In exchange for relinquishing some control of Gaza to Fatah, it seems, Hamas was hoping to receive badly needed financial help from Fatah so that it could pay the salaries of the public employees on its payroll.

In the end, the deal seems to have destabilized Hamas still further, at least in the short term. For years, Hamas had carefully balanced the need to project strength and credibility as the "Islamic resistance" with the desire to preserve full control over Gaza. In turn, Hamas has agreed to enforce cease-fires in Gaza when it was worried that an escalation might jeopardize its status as ruler, going as far as policing other armed factions.

The unity deal shifted the balance, temporarily tilting Hamas toward resistance. It is overly simplistic, of course, to argue that the combination of Egyptian pressure and the unity deal pushed

Hamas toward aggression against Israel; yet these factors did substantially change the group's calculations, with Hamas increasingly less focused on controlling Gaza and progressively more interested in positioning itself on the national political scene. This might help explain why the group met Israel's military operations in the West Bank with a rapid escalation.

Enter Egypt

If the way the most recent conflict between Israel and Hamas started is different from last time, so is the way it will end. In the course of the November 2012 confrontation between Israel and Hamas, Egypt took a direct and public role, pushing for a settlement. Morsi's government was not an honest broker—Morsi pulled Egypt's ambassador from Tel Aviv, sent his prime minister on a solidarity mission to Gaza, and threatened Israel in his rhetoric—but it was a responsible one. As the United States pressured Israel, Egypt leveraged its political influence on Hamas. Together, they brought the conflict to a relatively swift end.

This time, given the far more adversarial relationship between Hamas and Egypt's new president, Abdel Fattah el-Sisi, and the political and military actions his government has taken against Hamas in Gaza, it seems unlikely that Cairo will be able to deliver a cease-fire. Indeed, on July 10, U.S. State Department spokesperson Jen Psaki acknowledged the lack of influence the current Egyptian leadership has in Gaza, saying, "there's a difference between the relationship between the prior government to Hamas and the current government to Hamas."

Early Egyptian attempts to diffuse the hostilities between the parties reportedly failed, rebuffed by Hamas. On July 9, Egyptian foreign ministry spokesperson Badr Abdelatty tried to save face by arguing that Egypt was not negotiating an agreement but is simply attempting to end the violence on both sides. But the minimalist goals may have been the obstacle in the first place. Cairo initially sought a cease-fire deal akin to those of 2008 and 2009, a pure cessation of hostilities; but Hamas, less interested in following Egypt's lead this time around, proved unwilling to give up the political gains it was supposed to make with the 2012 cease-fire.

The 2012 Gaza war was an important test for Egypt's last president. So, too, is the current conflict a test for Sisi. The Egyptian president has openly stated his desire to be directly involved in restoring calm. Egyptian intelligence and security leaders recognize the detrimental effect of tensions on Egypt's borders. And so, Israel and the international community are watching to see if Sisi can be an effective partner. At an even deeper level, if Sisi can reach an agreement with Hamas, despite the vitriolic rhetoric directed at the Palestinian group from Cairo, it could also signal the new president's potential to reconcile with domestic political opponents that have been on the receiving end of similar rhetoric.

Given its regional status and historical role in brokering these types of agreements, there has also been significant international pressure on Egypt to play a productive role in the latest round of the Hamas-Israel saga. Last night, Egyptian officials tried again, floating a proposal that, on paper, would be great for Israel and good for Hamas. The parameters of the deal included not only cessation of hostilities, but also a gradual "opening of the crossings," a formula with some similarities to the 2012 deal. Israel accepted the deal this morning, whereas Hamas rejected it before even formally receiving the plan.

For Hamas, Egypt's involvement must go further than reinstating a simple cease-fire based on "quiet-for-quiet" between the two sides, while leaving political developments for future discussions. The recent proposal is strikingly similar to the 2012 agreement, which began to fall apart soon after it became clear that the promised normalization of Gaza would not be forthcoming. Stability between Hamas and Israel will require a long- term political approach for Gaza. Hamas could reasonably conclude that, if the sympathetic Morsi government could not achieve such an outcome, there is little chance that the anti-Hamas Sisi government would accept such a paradigm shift. And, to date, it is indeed unclear that they would.

The Near Enemy

Why the Real Threat to Israel Isn't in Gaza

Barak Mendelsohn

With Hamas busy firing rockets at Israeli cities, it's only natural that the Israeli public's primary concern in recent days has been physical security. But it should also be attuned to other, equally dangerous, problems posed by the current crisis. As Israel shifts to war footing, the authority of the Israeli state and the country's ability to remain a pluralistic democracy are under threat.

Following the horrific murder last month of three teenagers—Naftali Frankel, Gilad Shaar, and Eyal Yifrach—who were from Israeli settlements in the West Bank and were kidnapped and then shot by a Hamas cell from Hebron, anger and grief quickly turned into calls for revenge. Political figures from the ultra-right party Habayit Hayehudi (the Jewish Home) and extremist members of Israeli Prime Minister Benjamin Netanyahu's Likud Party demanded an immediate response, incitements that quickly echoed through Israeli social media. Ultranationalist and messianic elements within Israeli society predictably proved eager to answer the call. They were soon harassing and sometimes attacking innocent Muslims in the streets of Israeli cities and settlements—a wave of hate crimes that reached its peak with the heinous murder of a

BARAK MENDELSOHN is an Associate Professor of political science at Haverford College and a Senior Fellow at the Foreign Policy Research Institute (FPRI). Follow him on Twitter @BarakMendelsohn.

Palestinian teen, Muhammad Abu Khdeir, who was kidnapped and burned alive by a group of Israeli extremists.

As news of Khdeir's death spread, it seemed for a moment that Israelis had been shocked into recognizing the dire consequences of inflammatory and hateful calls for revenge. Netanyahu himself vehemently condemned the murder and any incitement against innocent Arabs, even as he drew attention to how Israelis and Palestinians respond to racially motivated violence. However, as has happened too often in the past, self-reflection—consideration about within Israel about the boundaries for legitimate speech and the state's monopoly on the legitimate use of force—quickly gave way to escalating violence between Israel and Palestine. Once more, conflict has distracted Israelis from the fact that radical, messianic, and xenophobic forces have gained significant ground in the battle for the soul of their state.

The angry rhetoric from Israeli leaders following the kidnapping of the three teens was not surprising given the nature of the crime. But beyond reflecting politicians' genuine feelings, it also appears to have been a calculated response to the difficulties that the government has faced following the April 2014 intra-Palestinian reconciliation agreement between Fatah and Hamas. Contrary to Israel's hopes, the international community, including the United States and the European Union, seemed willing to give Palestinian national unity the benefit of the doubt despite Hamas's role in it. The kidnapping, a clear challenge by the military wing of Hamas to the Palestinian Authority and to the reconciliation agreement, thus provided politicians a perceived opportunity to achieve a number of Israeli interests: to destroy Hamas' infrastructure in the West Bank, to undermine international support for the unity government, and to force Palestinian President Mahmoud Abbas to abandon the reconciliation agreement. Israeli leaders' harsh language was also intended to rally the Israeli public behind Netanyahu's government. After all, even the most ardent opponents of the settlements could not but sympathize with the horrible fate of three innocent boys.

But the politicians failed to control the rage and hatred they stoked, and their efforts backfired. The public's unrestrained anger and the subsequent murder of Khdeir diminished Israel's ability to mobilize international support against Hamas. Instead, these events focused worldwide attention on the radicalization of Israeli society. Some Israelis, including the chair of the left-wing Meretz Party, Zehava Galon, criticized Netanyahu and extremist politicians by drawing comparisons to Netanyahu's inflammatory rhetoric against former Prime Minister Yitzhak Rabin prior to Rabin's assassination by a Jewish extremist in 1995. And on the international front, Israel was put on the defensive in a renewed propaganda war.

Israelis should not be shocked that a combination of racism and fanaticism is spreading from the fringes of society into mainstream politics. It is the culmination of a long process. For over 45 years, the messianic movement has been an unrelenting advocate for settling the territories that Israel captured in 1967 (primarily in the West Bank) and preventing the state from accepting territorial compromises. Yet, since the 1970s, successive Israeli governments have pandered to religious extremists by extending financial and logistical support to settlements that were established without governmental approval, turning a blind eye to acts of Jewish terrorism, and publicly extolling the virtues of the messianic movement, rather than cracking down on those elements that disregard Israeli law by perpetrating acts of vigilantism and terrorism against Palestinians. Even the assassination of Rabin by a member of the movement did little to move the state to take on this domestic threat.

When Israeli governments began supporting radical Jews, they believed that the settlement project would help Israel hold strategic territory in the West Bank, strengthen the state's ability to protect its population centers, and, since the 1990s, enhance Israel's bargaining position in the negotiations with the Palestinians. Yet Israel's policy has failed to produce the expected strategic benefits. Rather, it has intensified the conflict with the Palestinians, reduced the state's ability to reach a peace agreement, and weakened Israel's international standing. At the same time, as Rabin's assassination demonstrates, it has deepened domestic divisions that threaten Israel's democratic pluralist identity and its internal unity. The attack by ultranationalist mobs on antiwar left-wing protesters in Tel Aviv this past weekend is just the most recent evidence of the severe stress that Israeli democracy is experiencing.

Even worse, the Israeli government has ceded so much ground to the messianic movement that Jerusalem is now unable to control it. For one, militant elements have penetrated the state bureaucracy and the armed forces. The military has become increasingly reliant on religiously motivated youth and on the rabbis they turn to for spiritual guidance. To some extent, the military now operates with a "dual hierarchy" system, in which religious soldiers are subordinate to both their officers and their rabbis. Radical religious leaders have not hesitated to use their newfound influence, especially as it pertains to the peace process with the Palestinians. On occasion—for example, when the state seeks to dismantle unauthorized settlements—some of the movement's religious leaders called on soldiers to disobey commands. This has hampered the Israeli Defense Forces' ability to mobilize for missions that conflict with Jewish messianic ideology, but the military has become so dependent on these people that Israeli leaders can no longer afford to rein them in.

The Israeli state has thus contributed to the gradual erosion of its own authority. In democracies, there are agreed-upon rules for competition over state policies, which allow actors within the state to pursue change. If efforts fail, the losers are expected to respect and submit to the outcome. But when they don't—and when the state fails to confront them—it risks losing control.

This is especially so in Israel, where ideological and religious commitments are necessarily strong. The authority of the Israeli state will always have to compete with ideologically motivated actors who flout the law—particularly those capable of skillfully manipulating symbols from Jewish history and Zionist ideology—for the allegiance of the public. Thus, the failure of the state to assert the primacy of its authority and laws is ultimately self-defeating.

There still remains a glimmer of hope that Israel will be able to halt the rising influence of messianism and the racist attitudes it has helped stoke, and reassert its pluralistic and democratic identity. Much of the Jewish public in Israel has not yet undergone an attitudinal shift in favor of ultranationalist religious ideology. Since the beginning of the second intifada in 2000 and since Israel's withdrawal from South Lebanon in 2000 and from the Gaza Strip in 2005 failed to offer the country security on those fronts, Israeli skepticism about the prospects of peace and the wisdom of evacuating any more land or settlements has increased. But most still support the two-state solution, which would require undoing some of the messianic movement's efforts and going against its core beliefs—that is, the total rejection of a territorial compromise.

Unfortunately, recent events suggest that a growing segment of the Israeli public is susceptible to fits of religious ultranationalism and could even be mobilized in support of Jewish fascism. These are bad omens for the future of Israel as a democratic state. The Israeli public seemed momentarily poised to recognize the immense danger of the country's current path. But with rockets targeting Israeli cities as deep into the country as Haifa, Jerusalem, and Tel Aviv, the threat of a third intifada in the West Bank and East Jerusalem rising, and demonstrations by Israel's Arab minority turning violent, the chance that Israel will make a serious effort to regain its democratic ideals seems small.

Bibi's First War

Why Benjamin Netanyahu Has Never Liked Military Conflict

Hussein Ibish

The best description of Israeli Prime Minister Benjamin Netanyahu's political style is that he is risk-averse. His entire career has been defined by careful calculation, caution, and a steadfast commitment to the status quo. Few in Israel seem to love him, but they do regard him as safe and reliable. And that has been a remarkably effective formula for staying in power in a country whose governments rarely serve out their full term.

Yet suddenly, Netanyahu has found himself well outside of his comfort zone. His government has been sucked into a major conflict with Hamas and other extremists in Gaza, and it has no clear strategic goal or even an obvious exit strategy. Netanyahu is thus in the very position he's least at ease with: he is at the mercy of events and other actors outside his control. He might hope that when tensions calm he will end up where he wants to be—the familiar status quo that he has always found politically comfortable. But that status quo, characterized by occupation and radical inequality in the Palestinian territories, is unsustainable and exceptionally dangerous for Israel, Palestine, and the region as a whole.

Netanyahu's remarkable rise to prolonged political power in Israel, particularly in his extended second term, has been based on his impressive ability to position himself between Israel's two poles: those who want peace with the Palestinians and those who

HUSSEIN IBISH is a Senior Fellow at the American Task Force on Palestine.

want to consolidate control over the occupied territories. He is a supporter of the settler movement, but not a rabid one. Settlers and their leaders have frequently accused him of "silent" or "de facto" building freezes, and his government has demolished a number of wildcat settlement outposts (although it has also recognized many others).

He professes to be a proponent of a two-state solution, but both his policies and his rhetoric leave grave doubts about his commitment to that outcome. At a recent press conference, Netanyahu undermined any hopes that he is truly open to a real two-state solution. "I think the Israeli people understand now what I always say: that there cannot be a situation, under any agreement, in which we relinquish security control of the territory west of the River Jordan," Netanyahu said, effectively ruling out the establishment of a truly independent, sovereign, and viable Palestinian state. In other words, his vision of the long-term future between Israel and the Palestinians is the status quo, defined by occupation and the rule over another people deprived of rights and citizenship, extended indefinitely.

Netanyahu seems content to leave things basically as they are, tinkering on the margins with new settlements and other small changes that may have a profound cumulative effect, but only in the long run. Anything else would be too risky. To restrain the settlers would mean a confrontation with the far right. To go in for annexation would provoke a massive diplomatic crisis. Netanyahu prefers, instead, to just allow the possibility of a two-state solution to fade away slowly, but inexorably. Indeed, in spite of widespread psychological speculation about the influence of his late father, a noted anti-Arab extremist, and his wife, whose cantankerous personality has been well documented, Netanyahu seems very much to follow his own counsel, which is apparently driven by a belief that the less done on major issues, the better for him.

Netanyahu does have some history of recklessness, but only when it comes to other people's fortunes. Supporters of former Israeli Prime Minister Yitzhak Rabin, who was assassinated in

1995, bitterly accuse Netanyahu of orchestrating a campaign of public vilification that led to Rabin's murder. And there is plenty of evidence that he did: Netanyahu appeared at rallies featuring posters of Rabin in Nazi SS uniforms and with crosshairs over his face. Netanyahu fulminated that Rabin's government was "removed from Jewish tradition . . . and Jewish values" by seeking peace with the Palestinians. Rabin warned that Netanyahu was promoting a climate of violence, an evaluation that proved apt when Rabin was soon after gunned down by a young Jewish extremist.

Another risky political move was merging his Likud party list with that of the far-right party Yisrael Beytenu in the last elections. It was a personal and ideological mismatch from the outset, and seemed to cost both parties at the polls. The merger recently fell apart, which has probably only reinforced Netanyahu's risk aversion.

With all his caution, Netanyahu has managed during his time in power to avoid leading the country in a major conflict. He was prime minister during a significant eight-day flare-up with Gaza in November 2012, but that couldn't be characterized as a fully fledged war in the same way that the current conflagration must be because it was short and contained, and Netanyahu always appeared to be in control of events as they unfolded.

By contrast, the current conflict seems to embody Netanyahu's deep aversion to unpredictable politics. It began with the kidnapping of three Israeli teenagers in the occupied West Bank by militants that were associated with Hamas but had quite possibly gone rogue. The Israeli authorities knew all along that that the teenagers had been killed soon after the kidnapping, thanks to a phone call that they made to the police in which their murder could clearly be heard. But the authorities withheld that information from the public in order to carry out a massive crackdown on Hamas in the West Bank, disguised as an effort to rescue the boys.

When their bodies were discovered after 18 days, Netanyahu's government seemed ready to call it a day. He signaled that he wasn't interested in a major escalation in Gaza; Israelis had been down that road before, twice in a significant way, and had learned that blowing up buildings and killing people doesn't change Hamas' behavior or the strategic situation on the ground. But because Netanyahu's government had deceived the public, the recovery of the boys' bodies unleashed a fresh wave of anger. When Jewish Israeli fanatics nabbed, tortured, and burned alive a 16-year-old Palestinian boy in Jerusalem, and then video emerged of the Israeli border police brutally beating his 15-year-old cousin, events took on a life of their own. Unrest spread throughout the West Bank and in Palestinian areas of Israel. The Israeli crackdown intensified. Rocket attacks from Gaza increased, and Netanyahu ultimately felt politically compelled to act, despite evident misgivings from the military.

And so now, for the first time in his career, Netanyahu finds himself presiding over the chaos of a war that seems very much outside his control. Hamas has launched countless rockets at Israel, including parts of the country previously beyond its range, and Netanyahu has unleashed an enormous barrage against a vast range of targets in the Gaza Strip, including the homes and neighborhoods of Hamas leaders. Israeli airstrikes have left more than 200 Palestinians dead, and the United Nations estimates that 80 percent of them are civilians. An intensified fear hangs over Israel as Hamas and other groups demonstrate the reach of their latest rockets. Although the Hamas rockets have been largely ineffectual, several Israelis have been injured and at least one has been killed.

It would've taken real courage, and a willingness to embrace political risk, for Netanyahu to listen to wiser counsel and avoid this pointless exchange of violence. It isn't clear whether Israel can achieve any major objectives in this war beyond killing people and blowing up civilian property and paramilitary installations, which is unlikely to achieve any major political or strategic goals and could do significant further harm to Israel's international and regional reputation. And the conundrum is made worse by the fact that Israel actually wants Hamas to stay in power in Gaza, both because Hamas is a known quantity that can be held accountable for its transgressions and because Israel fears the anarchy or the other, more extreme, groups that could rise in its absence. So Israel can go only so far unless it decides to, once again, assume wholesale responsibility for what happens in, and who controls, Gaza.

In recent days, a number of influential Israeli voices have advocated just that. On Tuesday Foreign Minister Avigdor Lieberman criticized Netanyahu's "hesitation" and declared that the current offensive should end with "a full takeover of the Gaza Strip" by Israel. Netanyahu responded by saying that he would ignore "background noise," a clear rebuke to Lieberman. And after coming under severe criticism by Likud leader and Deputy Defense Minister Danny Danon, Netanyahu curtly dismissed him. The far right continues to push for a major ground operation in Gaza, but Netanyahu seems determined to stick to aerial bombardments and small-scale ground incursions if he can.

As things stand, this conflict bears all the hallmarks of a classic lose-lose scenario, at least in the short run. Netanyahu might calculate that the price of being sucked into a pointless and bloody attack on Gaza was worth paying to avoid the political harm that would come from doing nothing in the face of enormous public pressure. But the risk- averse and cautious Israeli politician cannot be comfortable this week. The most Netanyahu can hope for is that when the dust settles the new normal in Gaza looks comfortingly like the old normal, something both Netanyahu and the Israeli public believe they can live with, at least for now. But with everything in the region in flux, that expectation may be unrealistic. In a worst-case scenario, Hamas could emerge from this conflict bloodied and battered, but with much greater political and nationalist clout and credibility throughout Palestinian society, including the West Bank, where the Palestinian Authority has been systematically weakened and looks utterly irrelevant and ineffectual.

Under Netanyahu's leadership, Israel is treading water, both in the Gaza campaign and with regard to the biggest questions it faces about its future. It is postponing the day of reckoning, putting off decisions about the occupied territories and the Palestinians, and pretending everything will somehow be all right. Avoiding the toughest issues, which most Israelis don't want to deal with and about which they share no consensus, may be an excellent strategy for Netanyahu's personal political ambitions. But it is a terrible abrogation of his broader national duties: making the hard and necessary decisions, taking prudent and wise risks, and putting the country's interests above his own political career and fortunes.

How Hamas Won

Israel's Tactical Success and Strategic Failure

Ariel Ilan Roth

N o matter how and when the conflict between Hamas and Israel ends, two things are certain. The first is that Israel will be able to claim a tactical victory. The second is that it will have suffered a strategic defeat.

At the tactical level, the success of the Iron Dome missile defense system has kept Israeli casualties near zero and significantly reduced the material damage from the rockets fired from Gaza. Israel's ground invasion, launched on Thursday, will also reap rewards. Indeed, it already has: Israeli forces have exposed and destroyed several Hamas tunnels, including some that were intended to allow cross-border activity into Israel and others that facilitated the movement of goods, ammunition, and militants within Gaza itself.

Such tactical achievements should not be minimized. But they do not equal a strategic victory. War, as Clausewitz famously taught, is the continuation of politics by other means. Wars are fought to re-align politics in a way that benefits the victor and is detrimental to the loser. But the Israelis have lost sight of this distinction.

In fact, Israel has a history of claiming victory when in fact it has suffered defeat; the October 1973 war is the best example. Israel claimed that it had won because its forces ended their war on the western side of the Suez Canal with Egyptian forces partially encircled behind them. The reality is that Egypt achieved the

ARIEL ILAN ROTH is the Executive Director of The Israel Institute.

strategic victory. All along, Egyptian President Anwar al-Sadat's objective was to seize and hold some territory in order to dislodge stuck political negotiations and, ultimately, recover the occupied Sinai Peninsula for Egypt. Sadat got what he wanted.

Israelis might believe that, even though they are not likely to see a political realignment at the end of this war, at least Hamas won't have achieved its own strategic objectives. The absence of large numbers of Israeli fatalities, the thinking goes, is a mark of Hamas' failure. But Israelis are wrong there, too. Killing large numbers of Israelis would be a treat for Hamas, but it is not vital to the group's definition of strategic success.

Hamas' strategic objective is to shatter Israel's sense of normalcy. It is only possible for Israel to exist as a flourishing and prosperous democracy under the garrisoned conditions of persistent conflict when its citizens are able to maintain the illusion that their lives are more or less similar to what they would aspire to have in London, Paris, or New York. With that illusion destroyed, several outcomes are possible, none of which are good for Israel. Despairing of the possibility of peace, small numbers of Israeli Jews may decide to emigrate. More likely is that disagreements over how to handle the Palestinian problem will deepen, sowing discord within Israeli society and undermining the core Israeli narrative based on the justice of Zionism. Cohesion around that narrative has been a key motivating force for making the sacrifices and facing the dangers that life in Israel often entails, including the long, compulsory military service that is a fact of life for most Israeli Jews. Although these internal fissures will not bring Israel to its knees, any erosion of Israeli power—including the power of the population's will—is a win for Hamas.

Israel has long been eager to thwart the expansion of the influence of Islamist resistance organizations that they see as determinedly more implacable foes. Consider that the first Intifada, from 1987 to 1993, led to the weakening of the secular Palestinian Liberation Organization (PLO) and to the rise of dangerous and militant organizations such as Hamas and the Palestinian Islamic

Jihad. The threat of these Islamist organizations motivated Israeli leaders Yitzhak Rabin and Shimon Peres to bolster the failing fortunes of PLO leader Yasir Arafat and embark on the Oslo peace process, which, had it succeeded, would have been a dead end for Hamas.

Indeed it was the violence of the second Intifada, which destroyed nearly 1,000 Israeli lives between 2001 and 2004 through wave upon wave of suicide attacks in the heart of Israel's major cities, which caused Israeli citizens' confidence to buckle and ultimately persuaded them to support a unilateral withdrawal of citizens and settlements from Gaza. They hoped the move would appease Palestinian wrath. It did not.

The persistent, low level rocketing of Israel's southern cities since Israel withdrew from Gaza has not caused enough disruption in the rest of Israel to bring Hamas any strategic benefits. In other words, Hamas' attacks on the border cities have not stopped most Israelis from going about their daily business in near-total obliviousness to the political and humanitarian condition of the Palestinians in Gaza.

This new round of violence, on the other hand, has caused enormous disruption. Rockets fired from Gaza have triggered warning sirens in Tel Aviv, Jerusalem, Haifa, Beer Sheva—all of Israel's major cities—and points in between as well. Those rockets haven't killed any people thus far, but they have sent almost everyone scrambling for shelter several times a day and shattered the illusion that what happens "there" does not affect life "here."

That would be enough for Hamas to declare victory. But the group has been racking up additional strategic benefits as well. First, the disproportionate number of casualties in Israel and Gaza has made Israel appear, at least to many Western eyes, as the aggressor, even though Hamas shot first this time around. Second, the Iron Dome has made covering the story within Israel boring for outside journalists. "Rocket goes off, rocket gets intercepted, life goes on" is not an exciting story. Israel's retaliations, which level Gaza's unreinforced buildings and leave behind mangled bodies,

Ariel Ilan Roth

sell more newspapers. And so, the world has focused on Gaza. Israel's friends may bemoan that as unfair—Israel is being punished for successfully defending its citizens, while Hamas leaves its own vulnerable. But that misses the point. War is not an exercise in fairness, but in the attainment of strategic objectives.

And, on that score, Hamas has already won. It has shattered the necessary illusion for Israelis that a political stalemate with the Palestinians is cost-free for Israel. It has shown Israelis that, even if the Palestinians cannot kill them, they can extract a heavy psychological price. It has also raised the profile of the Palestinian cause and reinforced the perception that the Palestinians are weak victims standing against a powerful aggressor. Down the road, that feeling is sure to be translated into pressure on Israel, perhaps by politicians and certainly by social movements whose objective is to isolate Israel politically and damage it through economic boycotts.

There are still those who will fantasize that this defeat will come with the same silver lining as Israel's loss in 1973. Although Sadat's attacks on Israelis in the Sinai shattered the feeling of invincibility that Israelis had nurtured since the end of the 1967 war, the war at least resulted in the Camp David accords and a durable, if cold, peace that has underwritten Israel's regional security since the late 1970s. Perhaps Hamas' strategic victory in this conflict will yield similar dividends for Israel down the road. However, such an outcome seems quite unlikely. Sadat had concrete objectives, namely the re- opening of the Suez Canal and the return of the Sinai Peninsula to Egypt—objectives that were reconcilable with Israel's own needs. Hamas, on the other hand, calls for Israel's elimination, an objective that leaves scant room for negotiation.

In the end, this round will go to the Palestinians, as did the previous major round of fighting in 2008. Focusing on tactical success should not blind Israel to the dangers it faces from these repeated strategic defeats. There is not much that Israel can do to change Hamas' behavior. What it must do, however, to prevent Hamas from capitalizing on its strategic success is to remind contemporary Israelis of what their early leaders knew all too well. As Moshe

Dayan, an Israeli army chief of staff and later defense minister, said, "We know that in order for their [the Arab] hope of annihilating us to die away, it is incumbent on us—morning and night—to be armed and ready." The challenge for Israel is to maintain that state of readiness while at the same time making the humane and appropriate choices that ensure its security, enhance Israel's attractiveness as a strategic and commercial partner for Western nations, and maintain its internal social cohesion over the long haul. This trifecta may seem impossible, but the first 19 years of Israel's national existence suggest otherwise.

Gaza's Bottle Rockets

Why Hamas' Arsenal Wasn't Worth a War

Mark Perry

Hamas' rocket fire into Israel has occasionally been described by the international press in dire terms—as a "non-stop onslaught," an "unbearable" and "incessant" assault that is "paralyzing the country" and making life "intolerable" for ordinary Israelis. One CNN report even claimed that Israeli soldiers were collapsing from the psychological trauma of the explosions. It has made for a nasty portrait of Hamas and its military strategy, one that could even be read as a tacit endorsement of Israel's stated goal of disarming the group with military force.

But a closer examination of Hamas' military capabilities and goals reveals a very different picture. Most of Hamas' arsenal is comprised of homemade rockets that are decidedly incapable of inflicting mass civilian casualties, flattening apartment blocks, or causing conflagrations that consume entire cities. "Hamas' rockets can kill people and they have," a counter-intelligence veteran of the U.S. CIA who spent his career monitoring Israeli and Palestinian military capabilities told me recently, "but compared to what the Israelis are using, the Palestinians are firing bottle rockets." Far from justifying the ground campaign in Gaza, the nature of Hamas' arsenal makes Israel's ongoing military operation entirely counterproductive.

MARK PERRY is the author of nine books, including the recently released *The Most Dangerous Man In America: The Making of Douglas MacArthur*. He served as unofficial advisor to former Palestinian President Yasser Arafat for seventeen years.

At the outset of the current conflict, according to Israeli Defense Forces (IDF), Hamas had 6,000 rockets deployed in Gaza, with an additional 5,000 deployed by its affiliate organizations, Islamic Jihad and the Palestinian Resistance Committees. Their combined arsenal is comprised of four rocket types: the short-range Qassam rocket with a range of 17.7 km (11 miles); the Grad rocket with a range of 48 km (30 miles); the M-75 with a range of 75 km (46 miles); and the M-302 with a range of 160 km (99 miles). The M-302 is by far the most sophisticated rocket in the arsenal, capable of reaching Haifa, which is 90 miles from Gaza City.

But even though Gaza has thousands of rockets, a large number of which can reach central Israel, Hamas' arsenal poses only a negligible threat to Israel's population. The vast majority of Hamas' rockets are unsophisticated Qassam types that are manufactured in Gaza in primitive metal workshops filled with lathes and simple tools. Although these rockets are capable of carrying a warhead weighing 10–20 kg (22–44 pounds), they have no guidance system and contain only a modest propulsion unit.

The IDF was clearly surprised by the reach of the M-302, one of which landed near the city of Hadera (about 100 miles north of Gaza) just prior to the onset of Israel's mid-July ground invasion. But Israel's response should have been tempered by the simplicity of the rocket's design. It had no guidance mechanism, its propulsion unit was modest, and it had a warhead much less lethal than the 175 kg (385 pounds) one it was designed to carry. Hamas, for its part, is very aware of these limitations. "We make up in numbers what we lack in quality," a Hamas official told me several weeks ago. "We know what we're doing. We can defend ourselves."

The IDF has carefully and publicly catalogued Hamas' rocket arsenal and its geographic reach, but has rarely offered a detailed analysis of Hamas' rocket firepower. For instance, during Israel's 2012 military operation in Gaza (known as Operation Pillar of Defense), the IDF publicized Hamas' acquisition of the Iranian Fajr-5 rocket, a sophisticated Iranian surface-to-surface system capable of reaching central Israel. What the IDF failed to note, however, was that the reason only a small number of Israeli civilians were killed in the conflict (five in all) was that Hamas' Fajr-5 guidance system was crude, at best, and its warhead nearly non-existent. In fact, according to the Hamas official with whom I spoke at the outset of the current conflict, Iran didn't give full- fledged Fajr-5s to the militant group, it only transferred the technology to manufacture them, a claim confirmed at the time by an Iranian military official.

The IDF's selective description of Hamas' arsenal continued throughout Operation Pillar of Defense, although for those paying attention, it was obvious that the rockets fired from Gaza were relatively unsophisticated and not very powerful. In November 2012, Gaza's al-Qassam Brigades announced that it had launched a Fajr-5 at Tel Aviv "as a response for the ongoing aggression against the Palestinian people," but the rocket did not reach its target. Several days later, a Fajr-5 hit an apartment block in Rishon LeZion, which is Israel's fourth-largest city located just south of Tel Aviv, destroying the top floor of an apartment complex and injuring two. If the Hamas rocket had carried a full payload, it is likely the entire apartment complex it hit would have been destroyed.

Hamas' arsenal is considerably weaker today than it was in 2012. The overthrow of Egyptian President Mohammad Morsi in July of last year has constrained Hamas' military capabilities. This is because it is no longer able to access large numbers of more lethal rockets as the new Egyptian government views Hamas as an extension of Egypt's Muslim Brotherhood, whose leaders the new military regime has jailed. Hamas has managed to smuggle some BM-21 Grad rockets into Gaza from Libya, according to Hamas officials. The BM-21 was originally designed by the Soviet Union for use on combat vehicles and was subsequently modified by the Iranian government so that it could function as a stand-alone weapon. According to Israeli reports, Iran arranged the delivery of this rocket to Hamas (prior to the latter's break with the Iranian-allied Syrian government) by breaking the rockets into four parts to ease their shipment to Egypt and then through the tunnels connecting Egypt with Gaza.

But Hamas has only managed to acquire a very small number of the BM-21 Grads. Prior to the Israeli ground operations in Gaza, it had no more than 200. Worse yet, the rockets have proven to be of limited use: Standing more than 20 feet tall, they are exceedingly difficult to maneuver and operate. They are also incredibly vulnerable. In the first few hours of the 2012 war between Israel and Gaza, 75 percent of Hamas' Fajr-5 and Grad rocket capacity was destroyed by the Israeli Air Force, according to a Hamas official with whom I spoke at the time.

Hamas' rockets have also proven vulnerable in the current Israeli offensive, in which the Israeli government claims to have destroyed 4,000 military targets in Gaza, which include Hamas' troop concentrations, command and control centers, and rocket launch sites. If prior Israeli military operations are any indication, the IDF would have had sufficient intelligence and firepower to eliminate two-thirds of Hamas' rocket capacity in the first 48 hours of its current air offensive. It's true that Hamas has nonetheless managed to continue its barrage of rocket fire on Israel. But the group is under few illusions that it is capable of inflicting any material harm. Instead, its aim has been to cause psychological damage and force Israel to negotiate by discrediting its military strategy, both domestically and internationally.

Although Hamas' rockets are of limited military use against Israel, Israel has allowed the rocket fire to rashly affect its strategic calculations. Israel has now focused its military campaign on the tunnels that allow Hamas to hide its rockets from Israeli surveillance aircraft, which include drones, helicopters, and F-16 jets. In public, the Israeli government has focused on how Hamas might use the tunnels to attack its citizens within Israel, but the IDF is very aware that the tunnels directly affect Hamas' rocket capabilities.

But the IDF seems not to have understood that, in training and deploying its rocket battalions, Hamas has modeled its strategy on other liberation movements. In November 1965, the United States'

1st Cavalry Division faced off against a number of North Vietnamese regiments in the Ia Drang Valley, in western Vietnam. What was important about the Ia Drang battle was that the Vietnamese had purposely lured U.S. units into a close-quarters fight, where the Americans could not use their artillery or helicopter-mounted missile systems. As one Vietnamese commander said in a meeting with a U.S. military commander after the war, the North Vietnamese tactic was to "grab you by your belt buckle."

Palestinians used these same tactics during the second intifada in April 2002, when militants battled the IDF in the streets of the West Bank city of Jenin. The Jenin battleground was a close-quarters fight in which the Israeli advantage in firepower was negated by having to fight house-to-house and street-to-street. Twenty-three IDF soldiers were killed, along with 54 Palestinians. The Palestinian Authority's president at that time, Yasser Arafat, extolled the Jenin fight as a victory, comparable in importance to Stalingrad. "It is Jeningrad," he said.

The Jenin model has had a powerful impact on the way the Palestinians have fought subsequent wars, including in Gaza. This time, Hamas' rockets are the lure. To stop the rockets (and unearth Hamas' tunnels), the IDF has been forced to fight in the streets and warrens of Gaza City and Palestinian refugee camps, thereby negating Israel's huge firepower advantage and leading to increased Israeli military casualties. In that sense, although Hamas' rockets haven't taken large numbers of Israeli lives, they've called into question the IDF's ability to defend the Israeli populace, choked off the country's most important international airport, and helped level the military playing field. But all of that has only been possible because the Israeli government has overreacted to what has always been a minor material threat.

Few in Israel or the West seem to understand the purpose of Hamas' rocket attacks. Killing Israelis is a secondary goal in launching the rockets. The primary goal is to change Israel's political calculations by creating the conditions for that country's international isolation. And for now, at least, it seems to be working.

Notes From the Underground

The Long History of Tunnel Warfare

Arthur Herman

P erhaps the most surprising development of the recent war between Israel and Gaza was the discovery of the sophisticated network of tunnels that Hamas had quietly developed in the preceding years. The dark, low-tech tunnels running underneath Gaza offered a stark juxtaposition to the modern artillery Israel deployed on the surface.

But if the tunnels hinted at an older kind of warfare, that doesn't mean they should be dismissed as a military curiosity. Compared with the most sophisticated weapons systems in use today, tunnels have withstood the test of time: for centuries, they have allowed military units to approach their enemies undetected and helped weaker combatants turn the battlefield to their advantage. There's no way to know how long drones or lasers or anti-missile defense systems will last. But as long as there is warfare, tunnels will almost certainly be part of the fight.

From Antiquity to Modernity

Tunnels and caves, tunnels' geologic predecessor, have a long history in warfare stretching back to biblical times. For at least 3,000 years, embattled populations have used them to hide from, and

ARTHUR HERMAN is a Senior Fellow at the Hudson Institute and author of *Freedom's Forge: How American Business Produced Victory in World War II.* Follow him on Twitter @ArthurLHerman.

strike at, stronger enemies. Ironically, this has been especially so in the region where present-day Israel and Palestine are located. Archaeologists have found more than 450 ancient cave systems in the Holy Land, including many that were dug into mountainsides, which the Jews used to launch guerrilla-style attacks on Roman legionnaires during the Great Jewish Revolt from AD 66 to 70. The Romans faced the same tactic around that time in their fight along the Rhine and Danube frontiers in Europe, against Germanic tribes who would dig hidden trenches connected by tunnels and then spring out of the ground to ambush the Roman soldiers.

But the use of tunnels hasn't been limited to insurgencies. It wasn't long before the Roman Empire began using them as an offensive weapon in siege warfare. By digging a hidden trench right up to a city's walls, and then tunneling underneath to undermine the walls and force a breach, the Romans discovered that it was possible to end a siege long before the city's population was starved into submission by blockade.

Unsurprisingly, perhaps, the use of tunnels in this manner soon inspired the development of countertunnels. The ancient Roman historian Polybius described a siege in 189 BC at the Greek city of Ambracia, where the Romans began digging a tunnel parallel to the city wall:

> For a considerable number of days the besieged did not discover [the Romans] carrying away the earth from the shaft; but when the heaps of earth became too high to be concealed from those inside the city, the commanders of the besieged garrison set to work vigorously digging a trench inside, parallel to the wall. . . . When the trench was made to the desired depth, they next placed in a row along the bottom of the trench nearest the wall a number of brazen vessels made very thin . . . [and] listened for the noise of the digging outside. Having marked the spot indicated by any of these brazen vessels, which were extraordinarily sensitive and vibrated to the sound outside, they began digging from within . . . so calculated as to exactly hit the enemy's tunnel.

This is a fine description of the use of countertunnels to intercept and disrupt a tunneling enemy's efforts. (It is also the first description of using acoustics to detect tunnels, a strategy that has become ever more sophisticated, although not necessarily more effective, over time.) The Persian Empire's siege of the Roman city of Dura- Europos in AD 256 led to another new development: when Persian militaries tunneling under the walls of the city hit a Roman countertunnel, they filled it with a poisonous gas made from pitch and sulfur to asphyxiate the soldiers inside—the first known use of gas warfare. The art of tunneling and countertunneling continued throughout the Middle Ages, with militaries constantly looking for ways to gain the upper hand. At the Siege of Château Gaillard (1203–04), the castle built by English King Richard the Lion-Hearted, French soldiers encountered three stout defensive walls. They eventually managed to break through because they found an unguarded toilet chute that emptied into a chapel inside the castle.

In the sixteenth century, when gunpowder was added to the tunneling battlefield, the results were literally explosive and increasingly lethal. European armies developed sophisticated techniques for planting barrels of gunpowder in concealed trenches in order to undermine or blow up enemy fortifications, also known as saps (hence the term "sapper" for engineers who did this kind of dangerous work). This technique reached a stupendous climax during the American Civil War at the Siege of Petersburg in July 1864, when Union troops surreptitiously dug a tunnel under Confederate lines, only to fill it with so many barrels of gunpowder that they weren't able to climb out from the resulting crater. In what became known as the Battle of the Crater, Confederate soldiers simply lined up around the edge of the tunnel and poured down deadly fire on their helpless foes.

By the beginning of World War I, tunnel engineers' main task was no longer to build tunnels to fortify cities, but to build trenches on the western front. The trenches were essentially a static system of tunnels that served as front lines for each side; it wasn't long before militaries began building tunnels in order to try to blow up the trenches belonging to the enemy. The British proved the most adept at this. At the Battle of the Somme in 1916, they successfully exploded two enormous mines underneath the German trench. In 1917, at Messines Ridge, the British military devised an elaborate strategy to dig 22 separate tunnels or mine shafts underneath German lines over 18 months. The Germans discovered one of the shafts, which had to be abandoned, but the other 21 were finished undetected and stuffed with 450 tons of TNT. On May 30, shortly before the explosives were detonated, the British General Herbert Plumer told his staff, "Gentlemen, we may not make history tomorrow, but we shall certainly change the geography." The explosion ripped the entire crest off the Messines-Wytschaete Ridge with a blast so enormous that British Prime Minister David Lloyd George claimed to hear it at 10 Downing Street in London. Ten thousand German soldiers were instantly killed or entombed. Plumer, however, was right. Although the British took what was left of the Messines Ridge, the war didn't change course. Instead, it dragged on for another year and a half.

Underneath the Good War

World War I brought three great innovations to the battlefield—the land tank, massed artillery firing high-explosive shells, and the airplane—that made armies feel increasingly vulnerable sitting out in the open. After the war, some military strategists responded by trying to put entire armies underground, in subterranean complexes connected by tunnels to supposedly impregnable casements and fortifications. The most famous (and the most futile) of these efforts was France's so-called Maginot Line, an elaborate underground system of bunkers and supply depots supporting 22 large, aboveground forts and 36 smaller forts, all connected by a railway, pulled by diesel- powered locomotives, that passed through a network of tunnels. In 1940, however, Germany's mobile blitzkrieg tactics completely bypassed the Maginot Line and France had all but lost the war before the thousands of soldiers in the fortresses could even fire a shot.

The U.S. Army built something similar, but on a much smaller scale, on the island of Corregidor in Manila Bay, with an 831-foot-long tunnel, some 24 feet wide and 18 feet high, feeding ammunition and supplies to a complex of artillery positions chiseled out of solid rock. An additional 24 lateral tunnels provided storage and sleeping quarters for troops. This was where U.S. General Douglas MacArthur, his family and staff, and Philippine President Manuel Quezon took refuge during the Japanese invasion of the Philippine island of Luzon in December 1941. But like its Maginot Line counterpart, the Malinta Tunnel on Corregidor turned out to be more of a trap than an impregnable fortress, as the new mobile warfare techniques of World War II left it isolated and useless. Today, both are little more than tourist attractions and symbols of military folly.

But around the same time that these massive underground complexes were being built, tunnels also experienced a revival as a tool for insurgents. The pioneers in this revival of tunnel warfare were the Chinese during the Sino-Japanese War, especially during the fighting around the village of Ranzhuang in Hebei Province in 1937 and 1938. Chinese guerrillas dug nine miles of tunnels between houses in the village to foxholes on the battlefield, so that they could attack Japanese soldiers from the rear. The tunnel entrances and exits were usually located in a house or in a well, making it easier for guerrillas to enter and leave without being detected.

The Japanese soon caught on, however, and began filling the tunnels with water or even poison gas. The Chinese retaliated by installing filtering systems that drew off the water and the gas. This cat-and-mouse game—which is typical of tunnel warfare—continued until the Japanese finally withdrew. How important the tunnels of Ranzhuang were to the battle's outcome is a matter of debate. To the Chinese, however, they are a monument to defiant resistance to the Japanese invader and, like the Maginot Line, are a major tourist attraction.

What the Japanese learned from the tunnel wars against the Chinese, however, would be invaluable in their fight against the U.S. Marines in World War II. They borrowed the techniques of hidden bunkers and emplacements connected by an elaborate network of tunnels, first on the island of Peleliu and then on Iwo Jima.

There, they turned an entire mountain, Mount Suribachi, into a honeycomb of tunnels and bunkers lined with concrete, with multiple exits so that Marines clearing one end of the tunnels would find themselves suddenly under attack from the other end.

Clearing the Japanese tunnels was a grim business. Facing Japanese soldiers determined to fight to the death, U.S. Marines favored flamethrowers, explosive charges, and hand grenades (according to U.S. rules of engagement, poison gas was not an option). Marines on Peleliu suffered twice as many casualties as Marines fighting on Tarawa, largely because of the tunnels; the Marines on Iwo Jima were still clearing tunnels two months after the island had fallen.

There was method to the Japanese soldiers' madness. They hoped that by inflicting as many U.S. casualties as possible—and making the United States' path to victory as slow, painful, and costly as possible—they would deter Washington from attempting a similar full-scale invasion of Japan's home islands. It worked, but not in the way the Japanese had hoped. In order to avoid an invasion, U.S. President Harry Truman chose to end the war by dropping atomic bombs on the Japanese cities of Hiroshima and Nagasaki.

Undermining the United States

The dawn of the atomic age forced militaries to dig even deeper underground to protect the chains of command from nuclear attack. So the United States built supposedly nuclear-bomb-proof shelters, including a five-acre network of tunnels buried under 2,000 feet of solid granite built into Cheyenne Mountain, Colorado, to house the North American Aerospace Defense Command; and the Presidential Emergency Operations Center, located 120 feet under the East Wing of the White House. Fortunately, neither one has been put to that ultimate test, although the PEOC was used by Vice President Dick Cheney during the 9/11 crisis.

But the most adept students of tunnel warfare during the Cold War were the Communist forces in the Korean and Vietnam conflicts. In Korea, underground warfare reached a new level of size and sophistication in the 1950s. To evade American air supremacy, North Korean and Chinese forces built underground fortifications so extensive that for every mile of military front on the surface, there were two miles of underground tunnels—more than 300 miles in total. The tunnels were built largely by prisoners, who ripped out more than two million cubic meters of rock for structures that hid not only tens of thousands of soldiers and supplies, but entire artillery batteries that could be wheeled out of mountain caves to fire on South Korean or UN forces (and then drawn back in to dodge subsequent airstrikes).

The tunnels dug by Communist forces in South Vietnam were nowhere near as massive as the North Korean version, but they enabled the Vietcong to maintain a guerrilla war for years against a more numerous and better-armed foe. The biggest underground complex was the tunnels at Cu Chi close to Saigon, initiated during Vietnam's Communist insurgency against the French colonial military in the 1950s. These tunnels extended some 200 miles toward the Cambodian border and came complete with ammunition storage, barracks, workshops, kitchens, hospitals, and even theaters for showing propaganda movies.

The U.S. military was so oblivious to the underground threat, at least at first, that in 1966 U.S. troops built a base camp—a 1,500-acre compound housing 4,500 troops—at Cu Chi, directly over the Vietcong tunnels. Black-clad guerrillas soon began organizing attacks on the base, popping out at night to blow up planes and steal weapons and equipment, including a tank, before disappearing into the darkness. The U.S. military responded by declaring the area around Cu Chi a "free fire" zone and pounded it with artillery, bombs, and even napalm in hopes of destroying the Vietcong. Yet the raids continued: from their tunnels, the Vietnamese guerrillas could wait out U.S. bombing raids and then prepare to strike again. The tunnels "were like a thorn stabbing the enemy in the eye," a Vietcong officer later remembered, one that had become impossible for the U.S. military to remove. According to one historian, the tunnels had allowed the Vietcong to so deeply infiltrate the U.S. military installation that at one point, all 13 of the base's barbers were members of the Vietcong.

When at last an Australian engineer revealed that the tunnels under the base were more extensive than anyone imagined, the U.S. Army realized what a hornets' nest it was sitting on. The effort to clear the tunnels included teams of Australians, Americans, and New Zealanders dubbed "Tunnel Rats" who entered small surface access holes barely two feet wide, usually armed with nothing more than a flashlight, a few grenades, and a small pistol. What they found was a vast labyrinth of communication tunnels leading to caves and caverns built at four separate levels. With nerve and courage, the Tunnel Rats defied the claustrophobic and cramped conditions—as well as booby traps, snakes, scorpions, hordes of bats, and angry Vietcong fighters—to clear the Cu Chi complex from the inside. At the same time, B-52 airstrikes pounded the tunnels from above, causing many to collapse. Some 12,000 Vietcong fighters were killed in the Cu Chi operation, but the United States had barely started securing the tunnel complex when the country withdrew from the war. Today, even the Vietnamese honor the Tunnel Rats as the toughest, deadliest foe they ever faced. (The Israeli military has a similar unit, the Samoorim ["Weasels"], as part of the elite Yahalom combat engineers.) Although the Tunnel Rats could not save the U.S. mission in Vietnam, they did write one of the grittiest, if largely forgotten, chapters in the history of the U.S. Army.

In Vietnam, the tunnel digging stopped with the end of the war (although the Vietnamese revived their use during the Chinese invasion in 1978). Not so in North Korea. After the Korean War, Pyongyang's appetite for tunnels increased. In preparation for a fresh invasion of South Korea, North Korea designed tunnel complexes across the demilitarized zone between the two countries. Between 1974 and 1990, South Korean authorities discovered four massive tunnels extending from North Korea under the border, each buried more than 100 meters under the surface and measuring two meters high and two meters wide—wide enough for three North Korean soldiers to march through shoulder to shoulder (sufficient for a full division of North Korean troops, roughly 10,000 soldiers, to march through every hour). One of the tunnels emptied out just 30 miles from the South Korean capital of Seoul. South Korean authorities closed down the tunnels as they found them, but no one knows how many more may remain undiscovered.

The Invisible Threat

The Israel Defense Forces face similar problems in Gaza today. In the IDF's recent incursion into Hamas-governed territory, it has claimed that it destroyed no fewer than 31 military tunnels leading into Israel. But there is no doubt that a large maze of tunnels still exists in Gaza.

These tunnels were clearly not the product of improvisation. Indeed, their size and sophistication suggest that, in recent years, North Korea has been providing Hamas both weapons and expertise in digging tunnels. The construction of Hamas' tunnels involved the removal of massive quantities of earth almost entirely with electric jackhammers operating some 60 feet underground, in order not to alert the Israelis. Then the surfaces of the tunnel were lined with concrete, and iron rails were installed down the middle to facilitate the transportation of soldiers, missiles, and weapons in—and kidnapped Israeli victims out. Some of Hamas' tunnels were large enough to drive a truck through, and nearly all were booby-trapped. They were also positioned so that detecting and clearing the tunnels would cause massive civilian casualties on the surface. Hamas' main underground command center, for example, is situated under a hospital.

What the IDF discovered, to its dismay, was that Hamas' tunnels weren't simply extensive—they were also jam-packed with weapons in preparation for an all-out offensive into Israel that Israeli authorities say was planned to coincide with the Rosh Hashanah holiday on September 24. If Hamas' rocket attacks hadn't triggered a bold Israeli reaction, including ground operations in Gaza, the tunnels might have gone undetected—and the coming Hamas offensive would have been as much a psychological blow to Israel as the 9/11 attacks were to the United States.

This is, of course, the great advantage of tunnels in warfare. They are an invisible and silent threat, unless you know what to look for and where to look. More often than not, countertunnelers have had to rely on luck, instinct, and human intelligence (that is to say, an informer) to find their whereabouts—and, as history has shown in Cu Chi and Messines Ridge, by the time they find out, it's often too late. Meanwhile, the factor of the unknown can gnaw at an antagonist's imagination, filling an entire community with fear and adding a dimension of psychological warfare to the other challenges tunnel warfare poses.

No one in Israel can be sure that the IDF has taken out all of the tunnels Hamas has built, any more than they know how many tunnels Hamas' Shiite counterpart, Hezbollah, has dug into Israel from Lebanon. Reports suggest that the Hezbollah tunnels may be, if anything, even more sophisticated. Likewise, South Koreans cannot be sure they've found every tunnel that their Communist neighbor has burrowed under the demilitarized zone, although no new tunnel has been found since 1991.

Technology versus Tunnels

Even the United States can't rest easy. The recent uncovering of more than 200 tunnels dug across the Mexican-U.S. border—95 in Nogales, Arizona, alone—has spurred fears of an underground assault. Most of these cross-border tunnels are used for smuggling illegal immigrants or drugs; but they could also become conduits for terrorists. That danger has prompted the Pentagon and the Department of Homeland Security (DHS) to develop new ways of detecting tunnels that are more systematic than relying on dumb luck or the occasional informant. In January 2011, the U.S. government even set up a Joint Tunnel Test Range at the Yuma Proving Ground in Yuma, Arizona, to sample the latest anti-tunneling technologies.

High-tech tunnel detection is an inexact science, to say the least. One underground detection expert, Paul Berman, has told the *Times of Israel* newspaper that electrical resistivity tomography, which measures levels of resistance in the earth under a given patch of ground, can find anomalies that would point to the existence of tunnels—or again might not. So far, no one has found the magic high-tech formula for finding hidden tunnels. "Tunnels have only been, so far, successfully located by intelligence, not by technology," according to John Verrico of the DHS Science and Technology Directorate. Seismic testing technologies that help oil and gas exploration or the construction trade find the geophysical character of a piece of land aren't designed to look for the distinctive features of tunnels. Sensors that work well in finding gaps or crevasses in one environment may miss significant features of another, including the presence of a man-made tunnel.

Ground-penetrating radar has been one promising area of research, using pulses of radio frequency energy to find voids or gaps beneath ground surface. GPR works fine for locating utility lines and minesweeping operations and finding buried historical sites. But looking deeper, to the 10- to 20-meter depths where terrorists like to lay their tunnels, is more difficult. Lockheed Martin is working with the DHS on a lower- frequency version of GPR, using electromagnetic waves to plot tunnels deep underground, but until now the results have been indeterminate.

Another promising approach is the prototype Active Acoustic Tunnel Detector, being developed at Idaho National Laboratory, which transmits up to 200 hertz of acoustic waves into the ground. An onboard motion detector measures how the waves move the dirt and rock that those sound waves pass through. If the ground is solid, the resulting graph shows a rapidly rising line. If there's a gap or void, the graph line will appear as a hump or dip. A third approach uses microgravity analysis, measuring minute changes in the planet's gravitational field to locate a tunnel. That requires a higher level of precision than current testing can show and will require a heavy investment in research to get any reliable results.

In any case, once a tunnel is found, there still remains the problem of how to clear or secure it safely, especially if it's booby-trapped. The use of robotic vehicles to explore and neutralize a tunnel structure may eventually replace the volunteer "Tunnel Rat." But for now, the old techniques of clearing them with explosives and a handgun remain the standard—as do the dangers of that approach.

In fact, if there's any certain bet to come out of the fighting in Gaza, it's that tunnel warfare in the hands of future insurgencies and militant groups will pose a persistent problem in spite of all the high-tech weaponry and gadgets of traditional militaries. Which side ultimately prevails depends on many factors. But anyone who thinks there's clear light at the end of this tunnel had better think again.

After Gaza

Why Withdrawing From the West Bank Would Make Israel Safer

Michael J. Koplow and
Jordan Chandler Hirsch

A s the latest battle between Israel and Hamas in Gaza wears
on, there are two schools of thought—one on the right and
one on the left—about what Israel should do next.

The first take, on the right, is that renewed fighting in Gaza
proves that Israel's disengagement from Gaza in 2005 was a mistake.
According to this view, the withdrawal empowered Hamas, inviting
rockets from above and tunneling terrorists from below, while earning Israel no international credit for having ended its occupation of
the coastal strip. That pattern, the thinking goes, would repeat itself
should Israel disengage from the West Bank. For that reason, any
pullout now would be dangerously misguided.

The second argument, on the left, is that Israel's mistake was
not that it disengaged from Gaza, but that it did not sufficiently
support the Palestinian Authority (PA) and its leader, Mahmoud
Abbas, thereafter. By failing to reward Abbas' nonviolent resistance, this theory suggests, Israel robbed Palestinians of the hope
that anything but Hamas' rockets could achieve their aims. The

MICHAEL J. KOPLOW is Program Director of the Israel Institute. He blogs at
Ottomans and Zionists. Follow him on Twitter @mkoplow.

JORDAN CHANDLER HIRSCH is a J.D. candidate at Yale Law School and a Visiting Fellow at the Columbia University Institute for Israel and Jewish Studies.
Follow him on Twitter @jordanchirsch.

best means of countering Hamas in Gaza, then, is to present an alternative in the West Bank and immediately return to negotiations with Abbas to demonstrate the efficacy of a nonviolent approach.

Both positions are understandable. Israel has fought a string of wars with Hamas since leaving Gaza in 2005, each more threatening to its civilians than the last. For that reason, maintaining some control in the West Bank seems to be the most sensible option. On the other hand, those hoping for more Israeli support for the PA would like Israel to bolster the notion that Palestinians can succeed without resorting to armed resistance. Yet closer examination reveals that neither of these positions is tenable. And, in fact, there is a third option. Israel correctly, if not faultlessly, disengaged from Gaza. And now, to protect itself in the long run, it must do so again from the West Bank. Israel must abandon the peace process in order to save the two-state solution.

Long Gone

Before Israel launched Operation Protective Edge, prominent policy figures within Israel had started reviving the notion of unilateral withdrawal from the West Bank. Disengagement, long supported by Ami Ayalon, the former head of Shin Bet, Israel's internal security service, earned the endorsement of Ehud Barak, then Israel's defense minister, in 2012. More recently, Amos Yadlin, the former chief of Israeli military intelligence, wrote a policy brief arguing that unilateral withdrawal is the only viable option to meet Israel's strategic goals while improving the prospects for future negotiations with the Palestinians. Meanwhile, in February, the former Israeli ambassador to the United States, Michael Oren, called for unilateral withdrawal should the peace talks led by U.S. Secretary of State John Kerry fail (which they did a few months later).

The most recent strife in Gaza, however, will likely silence these voices. For starters, Israelis widely regard their country's previous unilateral withdrawals as unmitigated disasters. The Jewish state's evacuation from southern Lebanon in 2000 emboldened Hezbollah;

the group portrayed the withdrawal as a victory and then amassed weapons rivaling those of a standing army, setting the stage for the 2006 war. Similarly, Israel's withdrawal from Gaza gave Hamas the space to create a terrorist enclave replete with rocket factories and attack tunnels into southern Israel. Given this history, many believe, an Israeli pullout from the West Bank would place the country in unbearable danger, exposing its heart to West Bank rockets.

These concerns are valid, but they rest on several flawed assumptions. The first is that all disengagements are alike. In fact, Israel's previous withdrawals failed for tactical reasons related to their specific circumstances. To begin with, the withdrawal from Lebanon took place following more than a decade of a war of attrition with Hezbollah, which led to a perception that Israel had been forced out in the face of armed resistance and increasingly bold militants on Israel's northern border. Given that no rockets have been launched at Israel from the West Bank and that Hamas' foothold there is tenuous, an Israeli disengagement would not be seen as handing Hamas a military victory. Israel would not withdraw from the West Bank in the same way it did from Gaza, either. When Israel left Gaza, it completely withdrew its forces and all settlers (albeit later maintaining, with Egypt, a blockade of Gaza's borders). It did not determine the withdrawal line for itself because the borders around Gaza were already set. A disengagement from the West Bank would be different in both respects, as Israel would determine precisely how far to withdraw and whether to leave security forces (and if so, how many) in the Jordan Valley. This would provide the Jewish state with greater flexibility to protect itself.

The second assumption is that, absent Israeli control, the West Bank would automatically devolve into chaos as southern Lebanon did and as Gaza did under Hamas. In Lebanon, though, Hezbollah already controlled the country's southern reaches before Israel withdrew and was thus perfectly positioned to solidify its control and launch another war. In Gaza, likewise, Hamas was well positioned to take over. The PA in the West Bank may be far from perfect, but it differs qualitatively from Hamas in terms of both temperament with regard to Israel and a willingness to refrain from rocket fire. In coordination with Israel, Abbas' forces have prevented the smuggling of rockets into the West Bank and the creation of indigenous weapons factories. Even so, some critics suggest, soon after an Israeli withdrawal, Hamas could simply oust the PA from the West Bank, putting Israel's population centers at risk from nearly point-blank rocket attacks. That possibility is not as likely as many would believe. Hamas' footing in the West Bank was unsure before Israel's efforts to root it out of the territory following the group's abduction and killing of the three Israeli teens in June, and it has traditionally proven stronger in Gaza than it has in the West Bank. In addition, since the West Bank borders Israel and the Jordan River, Hamas likely could not replicate the kind of tunnel system that sustains it in Gaza, nor could it easily smuggle weapons aboveground. Even if Hamas staged a coup in the West Bank or the PA joined its rocket war, the means to amass a Gaza-level arsenal would be limited.

The facts on the ground in the West Bank are also different from those in Gaza. Gaza has always been more crowded and impoverished. When Israel withdrew completely, it lost every last shred of leverage there—Hamas was not interested in negotiating toward a state, and there was little incentive for Hamas not to fire its rockets. In the West Bank, however, the economy is much better, the quality of life is much higher, and Palestinians there understand that they have much to lose in a large-scale Israeli military incursion. What's more, whereas Hamas had no interest in negotiations, the PA may prove more willing to discuss final borders following an Israeli withdrawal that would almost certainly leave Palestinians wanting more.

No Negotiations

The biggest fallacy in the argument against disengaging from the West Bank goes back to the heart of the debate—whether the 2005 withdrawal was, indeed, the right call. Israeli Prime Minister Benjamin Netanyahu's reluctance to now reoccupy Gaza hints that it was. Netanyahu, who resigned from the cabinet in 2005 to protest the disengagement, recently all but held his own cabinet hostage to ensure that no ministers went on record supporting a reoccupation of the territory. Netanyahu, it seems, has recognized that the true threat from Gaza is not rockets but occupation.

Hamas knows that it cannot destroy Israel militarily. Short of that, its strategy is to keep Israel bogged down in the territories and exploit the country's true existential crises. First, by keeping Israel in its current position of blockading Gaza and occupying the West Bank, Hamas weakens the perceived legitimacy of Israel's self-defense and exposes it to the increasing threat of Boycott, Divestment, and Sanctions campaigns and even to international sanctions. And by keeping Israel in the West Bank through its actions in Gaza, Hamas imperils the long-term viability of a Jewish and democratic majority in Israel. By maintaining its presence in the West Bank (or by reoccupying Gaza), then, Israel gives Hamas the closest thing it can get to victory.

Many in the center and the left in Israel propose escaping this dilemma by securing a peace treaty with Abbas. But a comprehensive settlement with the PA is as much a false hope as the reoccupation of Gaza. The last several years have demonstrated that Israel and the PA remain far apart on core matters, particularly Jerusalem, refugees, and the delineation of final borders. Simply put, Jerusalem and Ramallah have not yet found a lowest common denominator. And even if both sides somehow miraculously resumed where they left off—and did so with the full support of their parties and publics—the yawning gap of distrust between them would make a final status agreement nearly impossible. In the absence of any viable peace negotiations, disengagement is the best of an array of bad options.

Disengagement would create a de facto two-state solution, albeit an imperfect one. By withdrawing to the security fence rather than to the 1967 border, Israel would draw its own borders, incentivizing the PA to return later to negotiate a final settlement closer to its own preferences. It would also blunt international criticism of the occupation. Disengagement would thus allow Israel to alleviate, if not permanently solve, its twin existential concerns. Meanwhile, a withdrawal would give the PA a functionally independent state. This would allow it to discredit the catastrophic experiment of Hamas sovereignty and negotiate with Israel from a position of confidence. With this new reality established, both sides could postpone final border arrangements until a more suitable time.

A unilateral disengagement will not silence all the critics. To be sure, Israeli domestic support for another pullout would initially be weak, and the challenges of a disengagement from the heartland of Jewish tradition would be far more technically challenging and fraught than the withdrawal from Gaza. For the Palestinian public, Israeli control over large settlement blocs on the wrong side of the 1967 border will rankle many, as will an Israeli unilateral solution that does nothing to address claims of refugees and their descendants that have been harbored since 1948. The PA, meanwhile, may fear another Hamas-like takeover in the wake of a West Bank pullout and would likely object to any border demarcations that Israel made on its own.

The United States can and should help to overcome these legitimate concerns. Rather than foisting negotiations on Israeli and Palestinian leaderships that are not ready for a final status accord—and in doing so inadvertently raising expectations that could spark further fighting—the Obama administration should recognize that the time is not ripe for the traditional peace process. It can best foster the conditions for an eventual agreement by supporting disengagement now. Washington could ensure that Jerusalem coordinates its withdrawal closely with Ramallah by conditioning aid and security assistance for settlement evacuation on a smooth and surprise-free withdrawal. It could also offer Israel incentives to withdraw, including military resources to prevent the free flow of militants back and forth between Jordan and the West Bank and the acceptance of Israel into the U.S. visa waiver program. Additionally, it could vigorously advocate for Israel's disengagement in the international arena, to prod Europe and other powers to reward the pullout. Meanwhile, to win Palestinian cooperation, the United States could support Palestinian efforts, short of International Criminal Court recognition, to establish a Palestinian state in the West Bank. In coordination with other nations, it could launch a sustained Marshall Plan for the West Bank. And it could insist that the parties return to the negotiating table later to firm up final borders.

In the end, even if the worst fears of those who criticize unilateral withdrawal come true, Israel should still pursue this course. The recent fighting in Gaza demonstrated the efficacy of the Iron Dome system in shielding Israeli population centers from rocket attacks, and the technology will only be improved as Israeli engineers analyze the data from Operation Protective Edge. To address its security concerns, Israel is better off relying on such technical marvels than on an occupation that comes with added dangers. Israel thus faces this choice: address its international isolation and looming demographic takeover and manage security as best it can, or focus on security at the expense of all else. It would be smart to opt for the former.

Dangerous Disarmament

Why Israel Should Stop Pushing Hamas to Give Up Its Weapons

Benedetta Berti

On August 2, after 26 days of fighting, Israeli troops began to withdraw from Gaza. The move was soon followed by a full redeployment out of the Strip as part of Israel's acceptance of a 72-hour ceasefire brokered by Egypt, which could be a prelude to full ceasefire negotiations. In the past, any talk of scaling back has been met with public calls in Israel for continued military operations to defeat and disarm Hamas. But, these days, it seems that Israel is focusing on a more realistic exit strategy. Indeed, although eventual disarmament, demobilization, and reintegration of the combatants in the Gaza Strip would no doubt be a good thing, demanding disarmament and demilitarization without a long-term political solution to the fighting is both unrealistic and unhelpful.

Over the past few weeks, as Hamas and Israel sparred once more, there has been a growing awareness within Israel that the quiet-for-quiet formula—which is based predominantly on military deterrence and has guided relations between Israel and Hamas—at least since

BENEDETTA BERTI is Associate Fellow at the Institute for National Security Studies (INSS). She is Lecturer at Tel Aviv University and a post-doctoral fellow at Ben Gurion University and author of *Armed Political Organizations: From Conflict to Integration*. Follow her on Twitter @benedettabertiw.

Hamas took control of the Gaza Strip in 2007—has failed to provide Israel with long-term security. In turn, a number of political and security officials have suggested that Israel should settle for nothing less than a fully demilitarized Gaza. Israeli Prime Minister Benjamin Netanyahu has picked up the call, arguing during a mid-July press conference that, the "most important step for the international community to insist on" is "the demilitarization of Gaza." He reiterated that call again on August 4, insisting that the "rehabilitation of Gaza" should be linked to a process of demilitarization, a hint that this issue might factor into upcoming ceasefire talks.

The international community has followed suit. On July 22, EU foreign ministers issued a statement calling on all terrorist groups in Gaza to disarm. And in a speech last week, U.S. Secretary of State John Kerry stated that the group's post-war disarmament would be a key element in creating stable peace. Although "disarmament" and "demilitarization" are quickly becoming buzzwords in debates about how to end the conflict between Israel and Hamas, the notions are still vague and poorly defined. And that raises doubts about the purpose—and suitability—of disarmament as a goal in this conflict or as a pre-condition for a ceasefire.

For one, Netanyahu's repeated references to Hamas' future disarmament could just be good domestic politics, meant to help him win support from an Israeli public that has been demanding a forceful response and long-term resolution to recurrent wars with Hamas. In addition, pushing for disarmament also steps up the pressure on Hamas by signaling that Israel will not be satisfied with yet another temporary lull in the hostilities. Finally, Netanyahu's sudden calls for the international community to get involved in disarming Gaza came as the UN Security council upped its own pressure on Israel to end the war, and again after a ceasefire proposal written by Kerry was leaked on July 28 and was met with a vocal and very public outcry from the Israeli government. The Israeli cabinet interpreted the draft as giving equal weight to Hamas' demands and those of Israel. Cabinet members also believed that the agreement partially met a number of Hamas' core requests while relegating Israel's list of concerns (which included disarmament) to a vague mention of addressing outstanding "security issues." In turn, it seems, Israel upped the ante.

To be sure, disarmament seems unlikely in the absence of a larger and more extensive political process. And the international community and the Palestinian Authority security forces are uninterested, unwilling, or simply unable to enforce Hamas' demobilization. In other words, getting Hamas to give up its guns is probably not really the point. Rather, raising the possibility can be seen as a short-term domestic and international political tool—much like UN Security Council Resolution 1701, which ended the 2006 war between Israel and Hezbollah and endorsed "the disarmament of all armed groups in Lebanon," despite the fact that it was clear to all parties that neither the Lebanese government nor the UN mission there would have been able to enforce such a requirement.

But what about the long term? First, demanding disarmament as a precondition to a ceasefire agreement or for allowing humanitarian aid to be sent to Gaza complicates the current conflict, increases diplomatic tension, and worsens the humanitarian situation. Despite substantial military losses, Hamas can continue to fight Israel in the short and medium term. After all, as the July 2006 war between Israel and Hezbollah demonstrated, for hybrid militant groups such as Hamas, survival is the same as victory.

For Israel, the rhetoric about disarmament as a military goal can even be counterproductive. Operation Protective Edge had relatively specific tactical goals, including dismantling Hamas' tunnels and weakening its arsenal and military infrastructure. But insisting on "defeat and disarmament" could drag Israel into further military escalation under the ambiguous (and likely unattainable) goal of permanently ridding Gaza of weapons. In the unlikely event that Israel does remove all the weapons from Gaza, moreover, it would have to ready itself for a sustained presence in Gaza to prevent rearmament, an option with prohibitive international and political costs.

Given the perils of the rhetoric of disarmament, it would be well worth it for all parties to take a step back. Instead of pushing to raise the stakes, Israel should remain focused on its tactical goals and exit strategy. When the guns fall silent, Hamas' military infrastructure will likely be severely damaged. It will also be harder for the group to rearm, unlike after Operation Pillar of Defense in 2012, because of its tense relationship with Egypt. In other words, Israel has already achieved a substantial downgrade of Hamas's arsenal.

As Israel looks toward the exits during the upcoming ceasefire talks, it should also consider agreeing to the deployment of the Palestinian Authority's security forces in Rafah, which could help regulate the flows of weapons into Gaza. It would be a mistake, though, to put too much pressure on the Palestinian Authority and its shaky security services. Given the weakness of Mahmoud Abbas and his government, doing so could be the final nail in the Palestinian Authority's legitimacy coffin. It could also spark renewed internal strife in Palestine. In addition, the parties at the ceasefire talks should address the badly needed reconstruction of Gaza, linking assistance to sustained quiet, rather than to disarmament, and to working with both the Palestinian Authority and the Palestinian unity government.

Longer-term disarmament of the armed factions in Gaza has to be seen as part of a broader political process linked to state-building and economic development. Disarmament and demilitarization programs work when the broader population and militants decide that military activity is no longer necessary—that the political and economic benefits of peace outweigh those of violence. At best, seeking disarmament on the battlefield is an unfeasible political proposition. At worst, it is a path toward further escalation.

Is Trusteeship for Palestine the Answer?

Martin Indyk

In the wake of Hamas's coup in the Gaza Strip and the appointment of an emergency government by Palestinian president Mahmoud Abbas, the Israeli-Palestinian peace process faces its greatest crisis in years. A three-state solution cannot lead to a resolution of the conflict. Yet without a responsible Palestinian partner capable of living up to its commitments to peace, there will be no possibility of putting the peace process back on track. Given the collapse of the Palestinian security apparatus, the call is again heard for international intervention.

When I proposed an international trusteeship for Palestine in the May/June 2003 issue of *Foreign Affairs*, it was in the context of the forthcoming war in Iraq. At the time, President George W. Bush had claimed that a positive ripple effect would wash across the region. On the eve of the war, Bush had endorsed a road map for creating an independent Palestinian state. I believed that it was essential for Bush to take advantage of the opportunity that his war-making in Iraq would generate for peacemaking on the Israeli-Palestinian front.

But, having served as President Bill Clinton's and Bush's ambassador to Israel at the beginning of the Palestinian intifada, I had become convinced that nothing would come of any renewed U.S. effort unless an antidote was found to the fundamental weakness of

MARTIN INDYK is Director of the Saban Center for Middle East Policy at the Brookings Institution and was the U.S. Ambassador to Israel from 1995 to 1997 and 2000 to 2001.

Palestinian governing institutions. Without a responsible Palestinian partner and a capable and disciplined Palestinian security apparatus, no progress could be made on any peace plan.

Despairing that Palestinians could not on their own overcome the dysfunctional governing structure that Yasser Arafat had built, and knowing that Arafat was no longer a reliable partner for peace, I proposed a full-scale U.S.-led and U.N.-endorsed international intervention to take away control of most of the West Bank and all of Gaza from Arafat and the Israeli army. Those territories were to be held in trust for the Palestinians while the trustees worked with responsible Palestinian partners to create the institutions of a viable, independent state and while final status negotiations between Israel and representative Palestinians defined the state's final borders. The trusteeship for Palestine would have required an international force of some 10,000 troops—led by special forces—that would have been responsible for maintaining order, dismantling the infrastructure of terror, and rebuilding the Palestinian security forces.

Although this idea was considered by the Bush administration, the White House's appetite for trying anything similar in Palestine disappeared when its far more ambitious trusteeship in Iraq began to founder. Bush went back to his default position of disengagement from any serious effort to resolve the Israeli-Palestinian conflict, with predictable results.

With Gaza now firmly in the hands of Hamas, and Palestinian President Mahmoud Abbas gaining international recognition for an emergency government whose writ does not extend beyond the West Bank, voices can again be heard calling for trusteeship-like solutions. Indeed, the most notable calls for international intervention have come from the Israeli government, which had previously opposed the idea. Having pulled out of Gaza unilaterally in August 2005, with indifference to what would fill the vacuum, the Israelis have now come to understand the consequences: a failed terrorist state is being established on their border. Reluctant to intervene in Gaza again, they want some dependable party to assume responsibility there and help Abbas regain control. But there are no volunteers for taming a territory now teeming with armed gangs, warlords, and a well-equipped Hamas militia. The U.S. has its hands full in Iraq, NATO is struggling to meet its troop commitments in Afghanistan, and neighboring Egypt has no appetite for becoming Gaza's policeman.

Ultimately, if the ineffectual Qassam rockets that continue to fall on Israeli towns and kibbutzim become more deadly, that job may well have to be done by the Israeli Defense Forces (IDF). But once the job is accomplished, with high casualties on both sides, Israel will not want to stay one minute more than necessary. That is when an international force will be essential to help Abbas, as the democratically-elected president of the Palestinian Authority, re-take control there.

Meanwhile, Israeli Prime Minister Ehud Olmert, Bush, and the other members of the Quartet seem committed to preventing the West Bank from going the way of Gaza. They have responsible Palestinian partners in Abbas and his emergency government led by Prime Minister Salam Fayyad. But yet again, the entire enterprise is tenuous because of the absence of an effective Palestinian capability to control the territory. For the time being, the IDF is doing the job in the West Bank of dismantling the infrastructure of terror and preventing Hamas from mounting a military challenge to Abbas' control there. But the more Abbas depends on the IDF, the more he will be discredited in the eyes of Palestinians. One of their most pressing demands is for the removal of IDF roadblocks in the West Bank. But this will not happen until there is a security force capable of taking control—something Abbas does not possess. A U.N.-mandated international force should take over from the IDF and enable it to return to its pre-intifada lines in the West Bank. Abbas would immediately gain the credit for the Israeli withdrawal. He could then enter into negotiations with Olmert about the disposition of the rest of the West Bank, while Israelis have a chance to test the effectiveness of the international forces in the Palestinian territories.

The 2007 version of the trusteeship idea is perhaps better referred to as a "partnership" between the Palestinians and the international community, since the international force would not be replacing the Palestinian government but rather helping the Palestinian president take control of the West Bank as Israel withdraws in stages. Should Israel have to reenter Gaza, the same principle could apply. If Tony Blair is to have any success in his new job as the Quartet's Middle East envoy, he will need a game plan like this in his pocket and several thousand international forces ready to back him up.

www.ingramcontent.com/pod-product-compliance
Lightning Source LLC
Chambersburg PA
CBHW072249270326
41930CB00010B/2323